The Matrix As It Is
A Different Point Of View

Copyright © 2011
by
David E. Robinson

All Rights Reserved
Parts of this book may be reproduced subject to due
and specific acknowledgment of their source.

MAINE-PATRIOT.com
3 Linnell Circle
Brunswick, Maine 04011

maine-patriot.com

Do not accept the author's opinions in this book without verifing them personally for yourself.

We the People of the United States of America

The Matrix As It Is
Contents

Introduction -- 9
1 Our Founding Fathers' Motive -------------------- 11
2 Lawyers & The Law ------------------------------- 13
3 The Purpose Of The Constitution ---------------- 15
4 The Seizure Of The Americas -------------------- 17
5 Mayer Amschel Bauer ---------------------------- 19
6 The Founding Fathers Concede ------------------ 21
7 The 13th Amendment Set Aside ------------------ 23
8 The Constituted Trust ---------------------------- 27
9 A Corporate Fiction ------------------------------ 31
10 Converted Into Something Else ------------------ 35
11 The Sovereign States Abolished ----------------- 37
12 The Master's Will -------------------------------- 39
13 Title 18 & The Law ------------------------------ 41
14 The Democracy We Have ----------------------- 43
15 The Constitution Is Not For "We The People" -- 45
16 More About The U.S. Constitution -------------- 49

17	Abolishing The States	51
18	More Evidence Of Our Slavery	53
19	The Fraud Behind The License	57
20	The Use Of Trusts	59
21	The Debtor Is Servant To The Master	61
22	Facts Of The Mortgage Fraud	63
23	Under Admiralty/Maritime Law	67
24	Catastrophes, Calamities & Disasters	71
25	The Secret North American Alliance	73
26	The One World Government To Come	75
27	How It All Came About	77
28	Two Treaties Of Note	81
29	The King James Version Of The Bible	83
30	Power Centers Of The World	85
31	How We Americans Were Enslaved	93
32	How The Law Was Lost	101
33	The Robbers Of Today	107
34	Untoward Change	111
35	The Nondelegation Doctrine	113
36	What Must Be Done	119

"Do not believe on the strength of traditions even if they have been held in honour for many generations and in many places; do not believe anything because many people speak of it; do not believe on the strength of sages of old times; do not believe that which you yourselves have imagined, thinking that a god has inspired you. Believe nothing which depends only on the authority of your masters or of priests. After investigation, believe that which you have yourselves tested and found reasonable, and which is for your good and that of others' good." — Buddha.

Introduction

Science has taught us that, "for every action there is an equal and opposite reaction." If your life on earth resembles a Matrix, it is because you're seeing things for the first time with eyes wide open, but you feel confused. That feeling of confusion is appropriate because the information you are now digesting, contradicts much of the information you have been spoon fed throughout your life. This book is named after the movie "The Matrix," written by the Wachowski brothers. After reading this, watch the movie and you will notice many similarities.

My hope in offering this book is to help you, as the reader, make sense of it all, which will require you to wash your mind clean of the brainwashing you were subjected to by our government and our government controlled public schools and churches, and reeducate yourself. When you understand the actions, the reactions will make sense. Eventually, you will have a choice to make; a choice that will define: "How to survive life in The Matrix."

In 'The Matrix', however, nothing is real that your mind has been conditioned to believe is actually real. The Matrix is too big to defeat; no one can escape it, for we haven't the means or intelligence to beat those who are in control. Through research, we find that America is a society of nearly functional illiterates as far as the Matrix is concerned. This is not my opinion, I am only the messenger.

The people in charge of the Matrix represent the most powerful and intelligent people on earth. When gifted children appear in the public schools of the world, they are courted with scholarships, money and eventually memberships into secret societies. They will be introduced to very persuasive intellectuals who will convince these gifted young people that it is their place and duty to be a part of the elite who rule the population of the world because the rest of the world's population are too dumb to make decisions for themselves (the elite's comment - not mine).

When the "New World Order" is officially and openly in control, only the extremely intelligent will be allowed to propagate. Everyone else will be sterilized, or murdered through pandemics staged to eliminate excessive populations.

Every Foreign Revolution, the World Wars, the Depressions, Prohibition, Korea, Vietnam, the Middle East conflict, and the Influenza Epidemic during World War I, was planned and orchestrated by these elite people.

1
Our Founding Fathers' Motive

Our Founding Fathers' motive was partially centered upon themselves. Their personal ambition inspired them to accept the task of writing the Constitution of the United States; and not necessarily their patriotism. The United States is actually not a land nor a place: the United States is a corporation, a legal fiction that existed well before the Revolutionary War. (See: *Republica v. Sween,* 1 Dallas 43 and 28 USC 3002 (15)).

The Constitution of the United States was written in secret by the Founding Fathers and was never presented to the Colonists for a vote. Surely, any document as important as this document demanded the approval of the people it governed. Well, it wasn't presented to the people for a vote because the Constitution wasn't created for "We the People", it was created by the Founding Fathers, for their governors, themselves, their families, heirs and posterity.

The Constitution is a business plan, and any reference within it that appears to be the safeguard of a 'Right' is there because none of the Founding Fathers trusted their governors, themselves, nor each other. The safeguards were intended to prevent any one, or any group of them, from cutting out the others. Proof that "There's no honor among thieves."

Americans are no different from other humans who inhabit the earth. All human beings possess malleable minds that can be shaped and controlled; and when government shapes and controls one's mind, it's called "brainwashing." Brainwashing causes the subject to become 'functionally illiterate.'

In America, our functional ignorance excels in the areas of history, government, and law, which are really one and the same. Ninety-eight percent of the officials in public office are lawyers and these so-called "representatives" set policy and create the laws that govern this society.

Their use of Greek and Latin terms in law, and their habit of changing definitions and the usage of common words is intentional. The intent is to confound and confuse the general public, and to hide the treason they are implementing, so that members of the public are forced to, or decide to, hire a lawyer out of frustration, rather than try to represent themselves in our 'fictional courts of law.'

2
Lawyers & The Law

There has never been a law on the books created by Congress which made it illegal for a common man to practice law. Nevertheless, every Judge of a District, Circuit or Appeals Court, except Justices and Magistrates, is a lawyer and a member of the Bar. These Judges have the authority to establish local rules of court, and those mentioned have created a local rule that prevents common people from representing any other person in their court or 'to practice law without a license.'

A license requires that you produce your Bar Association number. For those who don't know, the Bar Association is simply a 'Lawyers Union,' and when lawyers are accepted into the Bar, they are required to swear allegiance to a foreign power. The American Bar Association is a branch of a national organization entitled; "The National Lawyers Guild Communist Party" and can be found recorded in the United States Code at: 28 USC 3002, § 15a. They have become so big and entrenched that they no longer fear reprisal.

Whenever we tell people that there is no actual law that makes it a crime to represent another person in court, their reaction is, "liar". We remind them that Abraham Lincoln and Clarence Darrow never went to law school or passed the Bar; but their reaction is understandable because the Bar is a very powerful organization and its members have infiltrated every nitch of American life and business. How many times in your life have you heard, "You can't practice law without a license?" We've heard it said in numerous movies spanning one hundred years; in daily soaps and by comedians in jokes and in theatrical skits. We've seen the phrase in print in newspaper articles, magazines, and heard it on the radio.

We all have been brainwashed to believe a lie because we've heard it so often from people we trust, who are supposed to have our best interest at heart; we just assume it must be true. How many other lies have you assumed, "it must be true?"

3
The Purpose Of The Constitution

Our American society has been lied to by their government and lawyers more times than you will sign your name in your lifetime, and we have been indoctrinated, "brainwashed," to believe that the Constitution was created for "We the People." The purpose behind these lies is to make us believe that we are free, safe, protected and secure, and it is all an hallucination.

How many of you have studied each line of the Constitution; the Statutes at Large, and the Articles of Confederation, armed with a reputable dictionary or a law dictionary from that era?

If you take the time to do this, you will soon discover that the true purpose of the Constitution was to create a business plan and to establish a Military Government for the protection of the Founding Fathers, the Kings commerce, protection of his Agents and for the future control of his subject Slaves.

Even the preamble of the U.S. Constitution is a clue to the lie and which states, "...to ourselves and our posterity."

If you never saw the title, "The Constitution," and you were never told what this document was about; what do you think would be your first impression upon hearing or reading: "...to ourselves and our posterity?"

The CONSTITUTION is not for "We the People" and AMERICA is a Matrix of misinformation.

In the eyes of those in control; America is nothing more than a large Plantation, and "We the People" are the Slaves.

In many U.S. and World Treaties the term "high contracting powers" is used to define your Masters. Everyone else is considered by them to be their Slaves.

All of the Founding Fathers had two things in common. They all shared the gift of a good education or were gifted individuals, and they all came from families of business and/or substance. These men all suffered from, "visions of grandeur." They viewed America as their opportunity to make themselves powerful and wealthy... "to ourselves and our posterity."

Initially, their plan was to steal America away from the King despite the fact that King George funded the exploration of the New World, which legally gave him first claim to all new continents discovered.

4
The Seizure Of The Americas

The seizure of the Americas by the King's explorers was not as it has been depicted in our history books nor presented to us by our government in government controlled public schools. Native Americans (the American Indians) were murdered, their villages burned, many were enslaved, infected by diseases brought from England, and their lands taken by force and the threat of force, by these early explorers. The Indians were labeled savages by these immigrant explorers from England, but the true savages were our English ancestors.

One thing the Founding Fathers did not know was that all of the King's lands and all future acquisitions such as the AMERICAS had been given and pledged by King John to Pope Innocent III and the Holy Roman Church by the Treaty of 1213.

After that fact was proven to the Founding Fathers, King George and representatives of the Vatican decided to use the Constitutional draft created by the Founding Fathers to further their plan to control the Colonists: control attained by bringing the Colonists to their knees in debt.

Any way you read it, the Constitution was never written with the intent of benefitting the American people.

Did you know that 98% of the Law Schools in America and England do not include Constitutional Law as a part of their law curriculum? The reason for this is because Constitutional Law does not apply to, or affect, the enforcement of statutes, codes or administrative regulations, which have replaced constitutional law, the common law, public law and penal law, and which have been designed to control you.

Constitutional Law is taught as an elective at Harvard, Yale and Cambridge, and only for students of law who are planning a future career in government. This should make sense to you as you read on.

In the true History of America, *neither side won the Revolutionary War.*

At first, the appearance of English troops in the Colonies was simply a show of force by King George intended to intimidate the Colonists and force them to pay taxes to him.

Factually; back in England, English soldiers refused to take up arms against the Colonists because they were English citizens and relatives as well.

5
Mayer Amschel Bauer

Mr. Mayer Amschel Bauer, founder of the Rothschild Banking Empire, by this time owned the King. Mr. Bauer had extended unlimited credit to the King and had arranged contracts with him which permitted the Rothschild Tax Collectors to represent the King and collect the King's Tax from the King's subjects. [This is the origin of the concept behind the establishment of the IRS].

It was Bauer who suggested to King George that he enforce a Tax against the Colonists in the New World, since the taxes being collected in England were barely enough to pay the interest to Bauer on the King's loans.

When English soldiers refused to fight, Bauer negotiated a contract with unemployed Russian/Germanic soldiers to fight for King George, at a cost of 50¢ a day. Bauer then informed King George that he had hired these soldiers in the King's name at a cost of $1.00 a day.

King George utilized these soldiers; dressed them in English soldier uniforms and ordered his career Officers to command them.

When this show of force in the Colonies failed, Mr. Bauer suggested that King George himself finance the Colonists in their War efforts against him and bring the Colonists to their knees in debt. The King succeeded in accomplishing this through his appointed civilian figureheads in charge of his government of France.

Mr. Bauer wanted to expand his Banking Empire into the Colonies. He discovered that the Colonists didn't trade in gold or silver but used script as the basis of their economy.

The script money used were promissory notes printed by the Colonists. All the Colonists had agreed that they would consider these notes to be the lawful currency of the colonies.

Mr. Bauer wanted gold or silver and induced the King to demand that his Taxes in the Colonies be paid in gold or silver. It was that condition "that broke the camels back" and resulted in the "Boston Tea Party."

"Whoever controls the money - controls the country." — *Mayer Rothschild.*

Surreptitiously, King George infiltrated the Colonies and their feudal attempt to form a new government, using spies composed of English lawyers and English aristocrats loyal to him. The spies' assignment was to infiltrate the new government, carry out the plan to defeat the Colonists through debt, and establish regular reports to the King.

The Church also had their appointed representatives in place to protect and insure that their interests too were being observed.

Much of the loans received from the French went into the Founding Father's pockets.

6
The Founding Fathers Concede

The Founding Fathers eventually conceded to King George's and the Holy Roman Church's demands by and through the intervention and persuasiveness of the King's spies.

Ironically, the common denominator, or glue that eventually bound together King George, the Founding Fathers, the English lawyers, and English aristocrats, was a secret society called the "Illuminati." Even Paul Revere and Benjamin Franklin were members of the Illuminati.

This secret society had had a criminal and deadly past in Europe, and in America they were eventually renamed "The Free and Accepted Masons". The majority of the regular membership of the Free and Accepted Masons do not know about the "Illuminati influence" within their rank and file. The Illuminati members operate out of special secret societies that are separate from the regular Masonic membership and are found in every branch of the Free and Accepted Masons of the World.

Think about the Colonists whom we have been taught to revere, by our public school system. All of these individuals were members of this secret society and all were traitors.

Our history books *also* instruct us to revere the Founding Fathers; but don't hold them in reverence, hold them instead in contempt. By and through their intervention, "Slaves you are and Slaves you might ever be."

An example of a man in history we have been taught to revere is Benjamin Franklin. Would it shock you to learn that he was on the King's payroll and his many trips to England were actually to report on the colonial government to King George?

The Declaration of Independence is another story omitted from our American history books. Of the fifty-one men involved in the creation of the Declaration of Independence twenty-one were actually traitors on the King's payroll.

During the Revolutionary War; English Officers were provided the names, addresses and family members of these thirty *loyalists* involved in the creation and signing of the Declaration of Independence. The English soldiers had been ordered to hunt down and murder all thirty *loyalists,* their wives, children and all relatives; with further instructions to burn their bodies inside their homes.

The soldiers were to leave no trace of these men and their families; to wipe out their existence for an eternity. The history of civilizations has taught us that *all martyrs are dangerous to men of power,* and King George didn't want to leave any martyrs.

It is not known who provided the detailed information about the thirty *loyalists,* their family, and addresses.

7
The 13th Amendment Set Aside

At first glance, it appears that Guy Madison, of Virginia, was so concerned about lawyers holding any position in American government that he championed the 13th Amendment which barred lawyers from holding any public office in government.

The original 13th Amendment was ratified but never made it into print in our government controlled school books for our public classrooms. The Amendment was surreptitiously removed and replaced by the 14th Amendment — i.e. the 15th Amendment became the 14th; and so on.

Madison's efforts appear admirable but his later actions as a member of the 1st Congress suggests that his only *real* concern was to block lawyers from undermining the theft that he and his compatriots had planned for America.

Once the cost of the Revolutionary War placed the Colonists sufficiently in debt, the English soldiers were ordered to dispense with their war efforts, recover their arms, and return home to England; which, within the next eight years, they did. The Colonists were so relieved to see the fighting stop that they allowed the soldiers to retreat, and leave America peacefully.

There is an old legal Maxim that states: "The first to leave the field of battle - loses." Pursuant to this Maxim, the Founding Fathers proclaimed the Colonists to be the Victors.

A Maxim is a legal truth that is time honored and incorruptible. In reality, *the War was just a diversion.* The Colonists had no chance of succeeding in their efforts.

Examine the facts for yourself.

During this era; England had the largest Army and Navy in the World. King George owned England, Ireland, and France, having a combined population of about 60 million subjects.

The Colonists were poorly educated, poorly armed and composed of farmers, tradesmen, bonded slaves, women and children, and boasted a total population of only 3 million subjects. And, considering the undermining that was occurring to their nation by the Kings spies and the Founding Fathers; the Colonists didn't have a prayer of defeating the English.

Americans have been indoctrinated by our federal and state governments — through government controlled public schools, and literature, government controlled media and government controlled churches [YES, EVEN THE CHURCHES] — to believe that America defeated the English.

We celebrate that victory and our so-called Independence each year on the 4th of July — and it's all propaganda; a carrot to lead the horse and keep this society passive and dumb. We boast today that our country represents the finest schools in the world, but in reality, we're no smarter than the first Colonists. We only know more about other things because of new technological developments during the last 250 years, and yet the average IQ of America is 70.

Documented proof that the Constitution was not for us can be found in *Padelford, Fay & Co. v. The Mayor and*

Aldermen of the City of Savannah, [14 Georgia 438, 520].

This was a court case wherein the Plaintiffs sued the City of Savannah, Georgia, for violating what they believed were their constitutionally protected rights. The decision of the Judge says it all:

> **"But indeed, no private person has a right to complain, by suit in Court, on the ground of a breach of the Constitution. The Constitution, it is true, is a compact, but he** [the private person] **is not a party to it."**

8
The Constituted Trust

The Constitution FOR the United States was converted into a Trust. A Trust is: "A legal obligation with respect to property given by one person (the donor), to another person (the trustee), to the advantage of a beneficiary (in this case the Americans)."

The property in this United States Trust includes all land, your personal possessions that you think you own, and your physical body. The donor of the Trust is the King of England and the Holy Roman Church. The Trustees are all federal and state public officials. This means that they are Agents of a foreign power; the Vatican and the King.

The Constitution was converted into a Trust because, *as a non-trust business plan,* it bound the hands of our government officials with chains. By their converting it into a Trust, our public officials were then free to make any changes they desired to the United States government without their constituents knowledge or consent.

The rules of a Trust are secret. No trustee can be compelled to divulge those rules. The rules of a trust can be changed by the trustees without notice to the beneficiary.

The one pitfall confronting them and their plan was the fact that by converting the Constitution into a Trust, our public officials had to legally assign a beneficiary; and the beneficiary chosen could not offend or be in conflict to the numerous International Treaties that were in force. Our public officials wanted to stay in control of the Trust as the trustees, however a trustee cannot *also* be a beneficiary.

So even though the Constitution was never designed or written for the Sovereign American people; they unknowingly became the beneficiary of this secret Trust, hence the creation of the "propaganda" regarding our Constitutional Rights.

All high ranking public officials, lawyers and judges laugh at the ignorance of those people who claim that their Constitutional Rights have been violated. Lawyers are actually taught to treat the members of the general public as subservient individuals. This also explains the "air of arrogance" that most lawyers convey, in their demeanor and speech.

The more powerful Agents of the states and the federal government, however, have been stealing the benefits from the Trust through numerous maneuvers that have the appearance of being legal while unlawful. In their defense, many former public officials (agents) were not corrupt to begin with, but by accepting bribes, or the consequence of enjoying an arranged extramarital relationship, they become victims of extortion plots and succumb to threats of being exposed regarding the bribes or their elicit affairs, to their constituents.

By becoming an agent, all is forgiven and forgotten. The people who arranged the bribes, also arranged the situations, and applied the pressure to force honest men to become dishonest. One example of this could be a sudden demand by a Bank to pay off a loan, based upon a hidden clause in the loan contract, which could result in a foreclosure, bankruptcy and scandal.

There are few remaining public federal employees in America. All employees who you believe to be a part of America's government are actually agents of a foreign government and this definition includes the President of the

United States. The federal elections are a joke. All of the candidates have been jointly preselected and prescreened by the National Boards of the Republican and Democratic Parties, well before the Election process takes place.

All of our federally elected officials, appointed administrators, federal police and Judges; receive their paychecks through the Office of Personnel Management. The OPM is a division of the International Monetary Fund, owned by the Rockefeller and Rothschild families and their Banking Empires, that operates in tandem with the United Nations.

The IRS and Interpol are owned by the International Monetary Fund, as indentified in a prior edition of the U.S. Army Manual, as a Communist Organization.

9
A Corporate Fiction

Those Americans who do not know how to assert their beneficiary status are treated by the government and their courts as corporate fictions. The corporate governments and their courts only have jurisdiction over corporations. Corporations have no rights or jurisdiction over living people and are only provided considerations that have been pre-negotiated in contracts by their directors. Otherwise, they're governed totally by commercial law, and so are you.

At this point, I believe I should address a "corporate fiction" for you by creating a situation you can relate to.

SITUATION: You've decided to go into business for yourself and you've thought up a clever name for your business. Everything you've read, and the advice received from a lawyer or friend, suggests that you should incorporate your business. To incorporate is to create a business on paper. It isn't real; it is a business in theory, which makes it a fiction. The lawyer or accountant you hired to prepare your corporation registers your business with the state as a state corporation and identifies you as its president of the board of directors; not its owner. Your business is now *"a corporate fiction"* and by recording the business as a state corporation, you no longer own it; it belongs to the state. You just gave your business away and made yourself a taxable state employee.

Our presumed government representatives have done the same thing to each of us. They changed each of us from "a sovereign" into "a corporate fiction." Your corporate name is easily identifiable; it is expressed in all capital letters on all your documents and on all the communications you receive from every government agency.

The reason for converting every Sovereign American into a corporate fiction dates back to the Principle of Law under the King. The King is a Sovereign Monarch and dictator, who by his authority creates the laws that govern his subjects. He is the Source of Law, therefore the law cannot be enforced against him.

In America, the Source of Law is the Sovereign People, therefore no laws can be enforced against them, as the Source, *except for those specifically agreed to,* or defined by the original Constitution FOR the united States of America. Such as Theft, Assault, and Criminal Mischief; but since the Colonists never voted on the Constitution, none of these *offenses* are enforceable against a living Sovereign. They are, however, enforceable against a corporation or corporate fiction.

In theory and according to the common law; before any Sovereign can be arrested for one of these crimes, a verified complaint must be filed with the elected Sheriff. The Sheriff, by his own authority, assembles a common law jury comprised of the immediate neighbors of the accused Sovereign, called a Grand Jury. The neighbors hear the complaint and consider the evidence presented to them by the complainant. They are permitted to ask questions of any witness and can subpoena anyone else who can shed light on the allegations. A majority must then decide if the accused Sovereign is to be tried by a court. All of this is done without a judge or prosecutor in attendance. This is a real Grand Jury proceeding, far removed from the joke perpetrated by our corporate government and courts today.

Our founders put grand juries in place as the ultimate check to the balance of official powers and they designed them well. Because grand juries sit for an extended length of time, unlike petit juries, it is much harder to seat them. Mostly they are populated with people who are older, often women whose children are grown, their husbands successful, with time on their hands and want to give something back to the community. They tend to be people who care about what they are doing and this is often a problem for prosecutors.

The grand jury is the weak underbelly of a corrupt judicial system, as it is outside of the control of the courts. Grand juries are, literally, a 4th Branch of government, not beholden to the courts, legislature, or executive. No one has control over them and that makes the public officials crazy. They have to utilize them but they can't control them. Grand jurors are *your* peers, not theirs.

What happened to our Grand Jury rights of old?

The Bar Association has successfully stolen those rights away from the Sovereign people, little by little, through re-writes of the Judiciary Act. Now the American people believe that the Grand Jury is an instrument subject to the jurisdiction, right, and whim of the prosecuting attorney. The prosecuting attorney controls the entire proceeding and who testifies. The judge then tells the jury what the law is and the members of the panel are denied the opportunity to view the written law.

All of our governments are corporations and are responsible for the creation of over 800 thousand laws called statutes, which are designed to control the Sovereign people of America. Just like the King; these statutes cannot be enforced against the Source of Law, which are the living, breathing, flesh and blood Sovereign people — *without their consent.*

10
Converted Into Something Else

All of the Agents in power, beginning with the King, the Vatican, the Founding Fathers — including now our presumed public officials — wanted to obtain power and control over America; but the Constitution prohibited them from achieving those ends. So they began to devise ways to change Sovereign Americans into corporate fictions. These Agents knew that they could not freely educate the masses without exposing their treachery, that our private and public education has to be controlled. So without any Constitutional basis, the U.S. Department of Education was formed.

The Constitution made it the responsibility of each state to educate their people, and several states challenged the Congress in the courts. The matter was eventually heard by the U.S. Supreme Court, which has never been a Constitutional Article III Court from its inception, which I will later explain. The Supreme Court ruled that the federal government was entitled to oversee the educational requirements of "United States Citizens" by virtue of the government's Constitutional powers to regulate Commerce.

Bad law is bad law, no matter how you turn the paper. That ruling gave the federal government the green light to initiate its "brainwashing" process upon the American public.

Let me explain how the Court arrived at its ruling because, these are not ignorant men. On every form you file to receive "government benefits" and even the "voter registration form," there is a question that asks: "Are you a United

States Citizen? YES/NO" and everyone circles the YES answer. Didn't you? Now look up the definition of *"United States Citizen"* in a reputable law dictionary. You will find that the phrase "United States Citizen" is a term designed to identify a "corporate fiction." Clever, isn't it? You and every other American had no idea that you were admitting that you were a corporate fiction when you circled that YES answer, and you did it under penalty of perjury.

11
The Sovereign States Abolished

The sovereign states had been abolished in 1790, by the adoption of Article 1 of the Statutes at Large which converted all the sovereign states into federal districts and gave the federal government lawful jurisdiction everywhere.

Considering the fact that the federal government is a corporation and that corporations can lawfully own other corporations — and that all American subjects have admitted under penalty of perjury that they are corporations — the Supreme Court ruled in favor of the corporate federal government. [All the more reason why lawyers should never be allowed to serve in government or in judgment of us].

Under our municipal and federal corporate governments, no Sovereign can lawfully be tried or convicted of any statutory (victimless) crime. I recently discovered how to avoid prosecution under the Trust, when a Sovereign is taken before a corporate prosecuting Attorney or a Judge:

First: the Sovereign must inquire if we are on the record, and if not, insist upon it. Say nothing, sign nothing and answer no questions until you are convinced that the proceedings are being recorded.

Secondly: all a Sovereign has to say for the record is: *"I am a beneficiary of the Trust, and I am appointing you as my Trustee."*

Thirdly: the Sovereign then directs his Trustee to do his bidding. *"As my Trustee, I want you to discharge this matter of which I am accused, and eliminate the record."*

Fourthly: if the Sovereign suffered any damages as a result of his arrest, he can direct that the Trust compensate him from the proceeds of the Court by saying; ***"I wish to be compensated for X- dollars, in redemption."***

This statement is sufficient to remove the authority and jurisdiction from any prosecuting attorney or judge. The accused will be immediately released from custody, with any check, license or claim he identifies as a damage. It doesn't matter what the action involves or how it is classified by the corporate law as either a civil or criminal action. It works every time.

12
The Master's Will

All of the Codes, Statutes, and Regulations throughout the United States constitute a "Will" from the Masters to their Slaves. A "Will" is defined as, "An express command used in a dispositive nature." When individuals in America are charged with a crime and warehoused in a jail; it is because they went against the "Will of the Masters" — not because they harmed another person. Remember that: "The Will" demands from us ALL that we are; keeps us in check, and promises us NOTHING in return.

The police officer, who arrested you, has been "brainwashed" into believing that he is doing the right thing, when in fact he is nothing more than an "armed slave" acting as a "henchman" hired to intimidate and bully all other Slaves into submission of the Master's Will. This statement will probably offend many police officers but this is a fact, and is not their fault.

Most police officers believe they are performing a public service, and doing the right thing in the performance of duty. They have been lied to by the government and in most cases, more so than anybody else.

Recently, the Police have all been ordered to complete paramilitary training, and were told that this is essential because of the new threat of Terrorism. The people responsible for this training, and brainwashing, are the same people [foreign Agents] who have been controlling us all since our birth.

NOTE: I claim that nobody told these police officers that

the suspected Terrorists might come at them from their very own government officials.

So our government officials now have our police officers training to act as a military unit, e.g., "Follow our orders and don't think."

They have succeeded in placing these officers on edge, so that their every reaction; will be an over-reaction to the situation, just like Hitler's Gestapo and S.S.

It is expected that police officers will over-react and begin killing innocent Americans, and once they are no longer of use, the officers and their families will all be ordered to receive vaccinations that will do away with them.

My guess is that after this planned mass genocide has occurred, the Russian and Chinese military will replace our local police officers in the field. Part of the Fraud perpetrated against "We the People" by this Will is the fact that there are actually no criminal laws in America. The Rules of Procedure used by every Local, State and Federal Court are Civil Rules of Procedure, not Criminal.

Court officials simply substitute the word criminal for civil, depending upon the case at hand.

Rule 1 of the Rules of Civil Procedure Reads: "There shall be but one form of action, a civil action."

This means that the Criminal laws promulgated and enforced by the police and our corporate governments are all civil and are being fraudulently enforced against our "corporate fictions" as criminal. When anyone goes to jail, it is for a civil infraction of the "Master's Will." That makes all of our jails, debtors prisons.

"Does this Ring a Constitutional Bell?"

13
Title 18 & The Law

Title 18, Federal Crimes and Offenses: was never voted on by the Congress; which means that these federal laws are NOT positive law in America.

Now, if you were a part of a government conspiracy to destroy America and soon to commit a mass genocide of its population; would you really want to vote Title 18 into positive law? It is my belief that the Congress intentionally omitted its passage so members of Congress could use that as a defense, should they be caught and tried for Treason.

Do you believe the lawyers hired or appointed to represent all the individuals accused of federal crimes knew about this fact? What do you think?

Armed with this fact: now look at the number of convicted people sitting in federal prisons who believe they have been lawfully convicted of violating a federal crime. How many do you imagine have been put to death? How many were shot and killed during the arrest? How many were killed attempting to escape from their illegal confinement? The Internal Revenue Code relies upon Title 18 to convict people of Tax Evasion, which only applies to corporations.

Look at all the people sitting in federal prisons who were convicted of this so-called crime? What makes it worse is the fact that the Queen of England, entered into a Treaty with the federal government for the taxing of alcoholic beverages and cigarettes sold in America. The treaty is called The Stamp Act, and in this Act the Queen ordained that her subjects, the American people, are exonerated of all other federal taxes.

So the federal income tax and the state income taxes levied against all Americans are contrary to an International Treaty and against the Sovereign Orders of the Queen.

Like it or not, the Queen is our Monarch and Master.

The Income Tax is illegal and still people have been prosecuted and imprisoned, contrary to law.

One hundred percent (100%) of the people sentenced and held in all American Jails have either been convicted of crimes that are not positive law, or were convicted of civil crimes, and are being detained by their consent. That's Right. The lawyers and judges representing our legislature and judicial system; created maneuvers to insure that anyone who is accused of a so-called crime, and posts bail, signs a contract to appear, and consents by that contract to the proceedings scheduled.

Anyone who applies for a public defender, signs the same contract without knowing it, and anyone who privately hires a lawyer to represent them in a Court proceeding, consents to the same contract upon the lawyer filing a "Notice of Appearance."

When you hire a lawyer, you signed a Power of Attorney. He is required to file his "Notice of Appearance" in that case and that "Notice of Appearance" offers your consent and binds your appearance to the proceedings.

Absent these aforementioned contracts; the Court cannot proceed against you. When that occurs; the Judge and the Prosecutor, attempt to trick and intimidate you into giving your consent. If you know how to invoke your Sovereignty, and refuse to accept what they throw at you and stand your ground, they will be forced to release you, after 72 hours has elapsed.

14
The Democracy We Have

We Americans are so proud of the fact that we live in a Democracy. Look up the word "Democracy" in a reputable Law Dictionary and see the legal meaning. Democracy is defined as: "A Socialist form of government and another form of Communism." Do you remember the lies that President Reagan, the Congress, and the Media, told America? That "The Iron Curtain fell without a shot being fired." The truth is that the Iron Curtain came down because Communist Europe found an ally in the West so there was no longer a need for walls.

P.S. Your Federal Taxes constructed the World's largest automated vehicle and munitions plant for the Soviet Union during the dismantling of the Berlin Wall.

P.P.S. The attempt to assassinate President Reagan occurred because he disclosed to the American people that "None of the federal income tax paid by the American people is ever deposited into the United States Treasury, and is being deposited into the Federal Reserve Bank for its benefit and use."

Shortly after making that statement, Reagan was shot by John Hinkley, who was quickly declared insane, so that there never would be a public trial. If you recall, President Reagan was never the same after that incident. The Masters don't play around — they eliminate problems or radically cure attitudes.

On September 17, 1787, twelve State delegates of the Thirteen State Colonies approved the United States Constitution, not the Colonists, and by doing so, the States became "constitutors." A "constitutor" is defined under civil law as, "One who by simple agreement becomes responsible for the payment of another's debt." [See Blacks Law Dictionary, 6th Edition].

Many early immigrants to the United States arrived here as Bonded Slaves. A person of wealth or substance became the *payor* by offering to pay or promising to pay or *guarantee* [bond] the debts of another person, and paid the cost of his or her voyage to America. This made the *payor* a *constitutor* and gave him title as *Master* over the *debtor* [slave] by written contract. A "Bonded Slave" is a corporate fiction. The *payor's* new title and power, as the "Bond Master" of the debtor, causes the immigrant to become a "Bond Slave" and property of the *Master* until such time as he is paid back his investment by the *Bond Slave,* or by someone else. This means that the *Bond Master* can buy and sell these contracts.

(That means you & me).

If a Bonded Slave is mistreated by his Bond Master, the law does not represent him because the Bond Slave — a corporate fiction, YOU if your name is in all capital letters — has no human rights afforded to him by any law.

Corporate fictions have no rights. If the Bonded Slave desires rights, he is obligated to negotiate them in his contract with the Bond Master before accepting the contract. If the Bonded Slave runs away from his abusive Bond Master, the law in place attaches a bounty, hunts him down and returns him to the Bond Master. Remember, the first Slaves in America were the Indians, and then Caucasians of English, French, Irish and German ancestry.

15
The Constitution Is Not For "We the People"

As mentioned before, the Colonists were never presented the Constitution, to vote on its passage and approval because the Constitution was never written for them, and has been rewritten two more times since then, but only our government officials knew about that.

And now, so do you.

1) Article ONE of the Constitution allows the Congress to borrow against the full faith and credit of the American people without end. It keeps us eternally in debt and makes all loans the government received from the King or any other entity, valid and enforceable against "We the People."

How is that good for us?

2) Article ONE, Section EIGHT, Clause 15 of the Constitution reads that it is the Militia's job to execute the laws of the Union. The Militia is a military unit something like the Police or National Guard, and is composed of members of our local community. The *new* State Constitutions, however, make Militias illegal except in time of war and authorizes the Police to arrest the members of a Militia, should they attempt to reform their ranks.

How is that good for us?

3) Article ONE; Section EIGHT of the Constitution gives the Congress complete power over the Military. What do

we do when it's the Congress who we need to have arrested for Treason and Peonage?
How is that good for us?

President Obama has changed the Military Oath. Soldiers no longer swear to support or defend the Constitution but rather to support and defend the President. Now, isn't that convenient — for him?

4) Article SIX, Section ONE of the Constitution is the law that makes American Citizens responsible to file income tax returns, not because of Title 26 of the United States Code. Parts of our flawed history, taught to you by our government controlled school system, accurately state that the English people had been taxed into a state of poverty by King George and this was one of the reasons the Colonists fled Europe for the New World.
So how is this good for us?

The IRS is NOT a U.S. Government Agency, they are Agents of a Foreign Power, operating under a private contract, and your obligation to pay and file federal taxes is a scam. Only federal employees and persons born in Washington, D.C., and the federal territories, were ever obligated to pay and file, prior to The Stamp Act, but we were never informed of that fact.

Our government has brainwashed us into believing that the National Debt is all our responsibility, and a patriotic responsibility to "pay our fair share." Here's the Truth about that subject.

The National Debt is a Federal Debt and always has been. The name change was the clever use of "propaganda" intended to invoke our patriotic civil pride. The foreign Agents in charge of our government have been borrowing funds with which to line their pockets, to buy influence, make business deals, and seal Treaties with communist Third World Countries and Dictators, which will never benefit "We the People."

They have lied to us, enslaved us, imprisoned us, and sold our gold to the Vatican in 1933, investing the proceeds for themselves. The money they have been borrowing since 1933, is not *real* money but, "negotiable debt instruments," which are the same thing as monopoly money. This means that in order to pay off the Federal/National Debt, all they have to do is print a money order without any account numbers on it for the entire debt, sign it, and present it to the lender — The non-federal Federal Reserve Bank — and the debt is paid in full.

The foreign agents who purport to be our public officials are responsible for eliminating the strength of the American Labor Unions, the elimination of our jobs, the erosion of our inalienable rights, and have instigated every war or conflict we have ever become involved with, in history, and convinced us that it was the other guy's fault. They converted us into corporate fictions, and sold us as securities to foreign corporate investors, and have stolen our heritage. Everything they have been doing is designed to undermine our freedom, liberty, and representative form of government. Their goal and final blow against "We the People" is the total conversion of our government to Communism.

16
More About The U.S. Constitution

The SIXTEENTH AMENDMENT to the Constitution, regardless of the dispute of how it was adopted, or whether it was properly ratified, permits the Federal Government to assess and collect a direct tax against "We the People." Most Americans do not know that the Federal Government is and always has been financially self sufficient, the result of tariffs imposed upon imports, exports, and commerce.

Not one penny of the Direct Federal Income Tax, paid through the IRS, is ever for or deposited into the United States Treasury. Those Taxes are deposited into the Federal Reserve Bank for the Master's use.

So how is this direct tax good for us?

You may be wondering about now, how the United States government can collect taxes from, "We the People," when we are Slaves, own nothing, and are not a party to the Constitution? Despite its legality, it is done under a process known as "debt collection" through private contractors [the IRS] and through a private contract, the United States Constitution.

The IRS belongs to the International Monetary Fund, who also owns the Federal Reserve Bank. The IMF holds the controlling interest in all the banks in America and throughout the world.

The IMF is the Rockefeller and Rothschild Empires, along with the eleven wealthiest families in the World. When you see or hear of a Bank closing, it is a diversion intended to injure and panic the public. The condition of the economy in the World today is being manipulated by these people. Their schedule for the adoption of the New World Order is close at hand and these public Agents need to scare us into believing that this new form of government is our salvation. Factually, it will only be good for them and it will be our ruin.

Article 12 of the Articles of Confederation promises the full faith and credit of the American people to repay all loans made by the United States government. The money borrowed by the United States to finance the Revolutionary War came from France. Who owned France? (King George.) Who was the opposition in the Revolutionary War? (England.) Our Founding Fathers promised our labor, equity, full faith and credit, to repay those debts that will, in theory, never come to an end.

So how is that good for us?

The Bill of Rights is not for your protection. They are laws that represent one man's ability, with the assistance of the State, to control another man's actions, and since they are included under the U.S. Constitution, they are not for you.

So how is that good for us?

The Thirteenth Amendment barred lawyers from ever holding a seat in public office. The Amendment was ratified. But during the second secret writing of the Constitution this Amendment was dropped and replaced by the 14th Amendment and the 14th Amendment was replaced by the 15th Amendment, and so on. The replacement wasn't done by a Constitutional Convention, it was simply omitted. The original Constitution is the Law of the Land and was designed to regulate our government.

The 13th Amendment still is positive law but now about 98% of our public officials are lawyers; so if we filed motions to remove them from office, who would sign them?

Wasn't that convenient for them?

17
Abolishing The States

On August 4, 1790; Article 1 of the U.S. Statutes at Large, pages 138 - 178, abolished the States of the Republic and created Federal Districts. In the same year the former States of the Republic, reorganized as Corporations, and their legislatures wrote *new* State Constitutions, absent defined boundaries, which they presented to the people of each State for a vote. Why this time? Because the *new* State Constitutions fraudulently made the people "Citizens" of the new Corporate States.

A Citizen is also defined by law as a "corporate fiction." The people were bound to the Corporate State, and the States were bound to the Corporate United States, and all of us were fraudulently obligated to pay the debts of the Federal Government owed to the King. This was necessary because the United States was officially bankrupt on January 1, 1788, and the politician's (our Founding Fathers) who benefitted the most by these Revolutionary loans, required a guarantee to present to the King. Absent that guarantee, they were *personally* obligated to repay the debts.

The state constitutions were rewritten again during the Clinton Administration, except now they are called the *Constitutions of Interdependence.* These Constitutions read just like the Declaration of Independence, except that "We the People" have been eliminated. This is the Magna Carta of the public officials, to protect them under The New World Order Communist Government. The public was never informed of this, like everything else, and the media never reported any of the Fraud being perpetrated against America by their public officials.

I could go on and on, discussing Articles and Amendments of the Constitution but suffice it to say that the "benefits" the government dangled in front of our "noses" have been used to induce us to volunteer, and all of these "benefits" are received at a terrible cost. When we apply for government benefits, the foreign government in charge converts our living sovereign person into a corporation and then records our corporate person as "government asset property".

The States used to provide protection, stability, and security for the people, but over time the focus of their attention has changed to the control of our minds, bodies, assets, and spirit. To take a loyalty oath to support, defend, and obey the Constitution *now,* is to swear an oath to your Masters to be ever loyal to them.

18
More Evidence Of Our Slavery

The primary control and custody of infants is with the corporate state government through the filing of government issued Birth Certificates, which are held in a State Trust; therein each applicant is recorded under the Department of Transportation as a State owned Vessel and financial asset.

A government issued Birth Certificate was never needed as proof of birth because a baptismal record, or a family Bible entry of birth, was and is an exception to hear-say, and constitutes legal proof of birth. Had your parents never applied for a government issued Birth Certificate, none of the Federal or State Statutes, Codes or Regulations in place, would be enforceable against you, and no government official or agency could ever tell you how to raise your children, declare you an unfit parent, or take your children away from you without your consent.

Many people made fun of the Amish of Pennsylvania, and yet the government cannot touch them because they do not participate in anything these corporate governments have to offer. The title to their land is recorded as an Ecclesiastical Trust. The Vatican (the Holy Roman Church) owns all the land, territories, and insular possessions called America, and as long as the Amish remain an Ecclesiastical Trust, and remain a passive Christian Society, the Vatican will protect them.

The Holy Roman Church possesses the power to protect or crush anyone and anything. (See: *Tillman v. Rob-*

erts, 108 So. 62 [and] Title 26 USC 7701 [and] 18 USC Section 8).

Social Security is not a Trust or Insurance policy or Insurance against disability. The U.S. Supreme Court has ruled that Social Security is a government giveaway program funded by a government Tax; which is why and how Congress can periodically dip into the assets of the fund anytime they want to and never have to pay it back. The back of the Social Security card states that the card is the property of the government and not you.

Your birth name appears on the front of that card, and has been modified, the same way as your birth certificate; from upper and lower case letters to all capital letters, pursuant to the U.S. Government Printing Manual, which instructs government agencies on how to subtly convert a living man into a corporation. The actual Director of our Social Security Fund and Administration is the Queen of England, from which she is paid a generous salary.

Your Social Security Card is issued by the United Nations through the International Monetary Fund, and your Social Security Number is actually your "International Slave Number." On the reverse side of that card is an Identification letter followed by eight numbers. This is a "cusip" identification number,* which is required on all securities. Yes. You have been converted into a marketable security, like a bond, and your person was offered for sale and sold to domestic and foreign corporate investors.

A Marriage License Application is a request to your "Masters" for permission to marry. If you ever had any claim of sovereignty before that date; you lost it completely when you applied for, and married under a marriage license. Sovereignty means: "To assert ones independence and to claim to be self-governing." The marriage license isn't necessary, and never has been, because a marriage has always been a contract between a man and a woman, witnessed by God. Who told you that you must apply for a license? The official you chose to conduct your ceremony? The official just happens to be a licensed government official, and his license prevents him from conducting marriage ceremonies without the issuance of a marriage license. Did Moses or Jesus ever say or profess that a marriage without a license is not recognized by God?

*CUSIP stands for Committee on Uniform Securities Identification Procedures. A CUSIP number identifies most securities, including: stocks of all registered U.S. and Canadian companies, and U.S. government and municipal bonds. The CUSIP system—owned by the American Bankers Association and operated by Standard & Poor's—facilitates the clearing and settlement process of securities.

The number consists of nine characters (including letters and numbers) that uniquely identify a company or issuer and the type of security. A similar system is used to identify foreign securities (CUSIP International Numbering System).

For more information about how the CUSIP process works, you can contact CUSIP at (212) 438-6500 or visit its website.

http://www.sec.gov/answers/cusip.htm

19
The Fraud Behing The License

Those who apply for, and marry pursuant to a marriage license have added a third party to their marriage contract. The third party is the Master, by and through his Agent, the Corporate State. The marriage license gives the State the legal right to decide the fate of the husband, wife, and the possessions they procure during their marriage. Should the marriage fail, their divorce must now be decided by and through the States' Corporate Court by a Corporate Judge; and the Judge's first and foremost concern is the "interest of the State." The interest of the bride and groom is now secondary. (See: *VanKosten v. VanKosten,* 154 N.E. 146).

A comment by the Judge deciding this divorce says it all: "The ultimate ownership of all property is the State: individual so-called ownership is only by virtue of government, i.e., laws amounting to mere use must be in accordance with law and subordinate to the necessities of the state." (Also See: Senate Document No. 43 of the 73rd Congress, 1st Session and *Brown v. Welch,* U.S. Superior Court).

The term "license" is defined in law as, "A permit to do something illegal." (See: Blacks Law Dictionary, 6th or 7th Edition). Therefore, all licenses are permits to violate the only real law. Inalienable rights are the rights bestowed by God at birth upon all living men. All other laws are subordinate to God's law. The controlling government wants us to rely on *their laws,* so they demand that we apply for a license. Another example is a "Drivers License." It is your God given right to travel the roadways of this nation, and no government has any right to restrict, tax, or license your pursuit of happiness. The only exception is a Driver of a Commercial Vehicle. The governments have a right to regulate Commerce, which means trade. Anyone operating a vehicle in Commerce must be licensed, but all others are absolutely free to travel without one.

The foreign Agents in power have changed the common meanings of words to capture and control every Sovereign. They succeed in this intimidation through the corporate courts and police enforcement by officers who have been brainwashed and reinforced by mandatory training programs.

20
The Use Of Trusts

The use of "Trusts" by the Masters and their Agents is for a good reason. A Trust by law is secret; neither the Masters nor their agents (the Corporate Government and Courts) can be compelled to expose the rules or regulations of the Trust, and those regulations can change, without notice to the participants. (See: The Law of Trusts).

Slaves (meaning you) cannot own property. Look at the Deed to your home. You are identified as the Tenant of the property; never the Owner. Your Local and State land tax is actually a "rent" or "use fee" assessed by the State for your lease on the land. You gave them the land upon closing on the deed, via your Lawyer. Did he ever tell you that? After closing, your Lawyer recorded the deed with the County. The law only *suggests* recording the deed, it doesn't mandate it. Upon recording the deed, you give the land back to the State, who then leases it back to you, for as long as you live there. Isn't that where you have constructed your castle, your home?

"I'm paying for it, doesn't that make the land mine?" you ask. If you fail to pay the State's assessed "rent" or "use fee" — which is a cleverly disguised State direct tax — you will be evicted from your castle and land, and the State will take title to, and sell your home under commercial law.

Commercial Law ordains that, "Anything permanently attached, is retained by the owner." Who is the owner of the land? Why the State, because you so graciously gave it to them. Oh, I almost forgot, your Lawyer receives a fee from the State for recording your deed for their benefit and use. How do you feel about your lawyer now? Didn't you pay him to represent "your interests" at the closing? Now you see why lawyers are the brunt of numerous jokes and have such a poor reputation. It's because they deserve it.

Foreclosures are nothing more than evictions, based on a different kind of fraud: The illusion of a debt [a Mortgage] that never existed. No individual or family who has been foreclosed upon, and evicted from their home, in the United States, has been treated lawfully.

The people who purchased their homes through a Mortgage Company actually owned their homes "completely" on the day of the closing. The real legal definition of a "closing" means that all legal interest as to title is concluded. (See: any reputable Dictionary from the 1800's).

The definition has been changed by our government lawyers to conceal the fraud.

21
The Debtor Is Servant To The Master

First, you must know that the federal government took America off the gold standard in 1933, during a staged bankruptcy called the "Great Depression", and replaced the gold with "Negotiable Debt Instruments." (YES, THE GREAT DEPRESSION WAS STAGED). The government needed to create a crisis to implement standards designed to steal your possessions and God-given rights.

The process of creating a crisis was discovered by behaviorists. Take away a person's food, comfort, and safety, long enough, and he won't care about, or question the illusion provided, as long as his stomach is full, he has shelter, a comfortable bed, and the means (real or imagined) to keep or continue his comfort.

President Roosevelt unconstitutionally collected America's gold by Executive Order and sold it to the Vatican at a profit, by way of China, to conceal its true ownership. The gold in Fort Knox belongs to the Vatican; not to the United States. Absent a gold base, Commerce now essentially trades in "debt." So if you borrowed money for a Mortgage, and there is no gold or real value to support the paper called U.S. Currency, what did you actually borrow?

Factually, you borrowed "debt." The Mortgage Company committed the ultimate fraud against you because they loaned you nothing, to pay off the imaginary balance, not even their own debt instruments. They then told you that you owe them the unpaid balance of your home, and that you must pay them back in monthly installments, with interest.

22
Facts Of The Mortgage Fraud

At your Closing, the Mortgage Company had you sign a "Promissory Note" in which you promised your sweat, your equity, your full faith and credit against an unpaid balance. Then, without your knowledge or consent, the Mortgage Company sold your Promissory Note (your credit) to a Warehousing Institution, such as Fannie Mae or Freddie Mac.

The Warehousing Institution uses your Promissory Note (your credit) as collateral, and generates loans to other people and corporations, at interest. Collateral is essential to a corporation because corporations have no money or credit. They're not real, they're a fiction and require the sweat, the equity, and the full faith and credit of living individuals who breathe, to sustain the life of the corporation.

Corporate Governments operate under the same principle. The Warehousing Institution makes money off the "Promissory Note" (your credit) and even though the profits made are nothing more than new Negotiable Debt Instruments, those instruments still have buying power in a Negotiable Debt Economy. These debt instruments are only negotiable because of the human ignorance of the American people, and the human ignorance of people in other countries of the World, who have all been lied to, told this has value, and the people don't know the difference.

Did you ever give your permission to the Mortgage Company to sell your credit? So where is your cut of the profits? If the Mortgage Company invested nothing of their own in the purchase of your home, why are you making a monthly

Mortgage payment to them, with interest? And where do they get off foreclosing on, or against anyone, or threatening to foreclose? They do it by fraud and the Masters and their Agents (the governments, the courts, and the super banks) all know it.

Everything done to us, and against us, is about sustaining their lives, the lives of the corporate governments they command; to keep "We the People" under their complete control.

They accomplish this control by taking away, or threatening to take away, your comfort and independence. They use fraudulent means, disguised as law.

Note: When you applied for a Mortgage, the Mortgage Company ran a credit check on you, and if you had a blemish on your credit record, they charged you points (money) to ease their pain, and lighten the risk (a credit risk) of their loaning you a Mortgage. More Fraud.

Why are you paying points, when they never loaned you a dime. The credit report is just another scam. If you have a high credit report, the government and banks identify you as an "Obedient Slave" and yet your "Promissory Note" sold for the same value as the "Promissory Note" endorsed by the man who is a credit risk. Credit didn't matter. The fact that you are a living person is what matters.

More Fraud:

The Mortgage Company maintains two sets of books regarding your Mortgage payments. The local set of books, is a record that they loaned you money and that you agreed to repay that money, with interest, each month. The second set of books is maintained in another State office, usually a super Bank, because the Mortgage Companies usually sell your loan contract to a super Bank and agree to monitor the monthly payments in order to conceal the fraud.

In the second set of books, your monthly Mortgage Payment is recorded by the bank as a savings deposit, because there is no real loan. When you pay off the fraudulent mortgage, the Bank waits (90) days and then submits a request to the IRS. The request states: "That someone, unknown to this facility; deposited this money into our facility and has abandoned it. May we keep the deposit?"

The IRS always gives their permission to the bank to keep the deposit, and your hard earned money just feathered the nest of the Rockefeller, Rothschild, and eleven other wealthy families in the world.

Equity Law, which once controlled America's Corporate Courts, has been replaced with Admiralty/Maritime Law, pursuant to Title 28 of the United States Code, and the Judiciary Act of 1789.

Admiralty/Maritime Law is the Law of Merchants and Sailors.

23
Under Admiralty/Maritime Law

Under Admiralty/Maritime Law, the Courts presume that you owe the Mortgage or the Tax, or that you committed a crime defined as a Criminal Statute, and it is your obligation to prove that you are innocent. This means that you are guilty until you prove that you are innocent; the same standard and procedure used in a Military Court Martial. Haven't we always been told, "You are innocent until proven guilty?" Lies, Lies, and more Lies.

We are not free men; we are slaves, bound to our Masters by adhesion contracts, and secret Trusts. The goal of the Masters, and their (agents), our elected officials, is to keep the people oppressed and subservient to them.

As the Masters' agents, they use propaganda techniques, through government controlled schools; churches; the media; and mind control by force, or the threat of force through the courts and police enforcement.

Police officers in America have been pumped full of propaganda, and because of their trust, public school conditioning, and training, they do not see what is going on. Many have been conditioned, by prior military service, not to think for themselves, but to just follow orders, which makes many of them as dangerous as a Terrorist.

Now ask yourself, who are the real Terrorists in America?

Guess what, "the Constitution isn't for the Police either", and still they are forced to swear an oath to defend it. The more regulations, statutes, and codes created, and the greater the number of regulatory officers and agencies to enforce them, the greater the Masters' control over their Slaves, by force and threat of force, by the very people we rely on "to protect and serve."

At some point in history the foreign Agents in control of our Federal Government, decided that they needed to create Federal Police Agencies to protect them. I can't blame them. If I was a part of a conspiracy that could result in the American people hanging me for Treason, I'd want bodyguards too. Now, if you are one of these public officials, how do you justify the employment and expense of bodyguards, when nobody is trying to injure you, and you don't want anyone to know that you are committing Treason? Instead of confessing your motives, you must find a way to accomplish your objective and blame it on someone else.

HENCE: The birth of a bad law, The Volstead Act, and the beginning of "Prohibition."

Enterprising people began to make money and others organized. Those who organized became mobs and when the mobs began killing each other, the free lance bootleggers, and innocent people, in drive by shootings; our federal officials sat back and enjoyed the show.

They did absolutely nothing until the public was literally breaking down the doors of the Capitol Building: Just as they had planned.

The FBI existed before this time. They were a small investigative unit under the Attorney General's Office. The Agents had no arrest powers and were prohibited from carrying guns. Their only authority was to investigate federal employees, and make reports to the Attorney General, who decided if the matter was serious enough to concern the government, and whether to prosecute the employee. The FBI was eventually armed, expanded, and provided with national jurisdiction to fight the gangsters. None of which would have been necessary had it not been for The Volstead Act.

Slowly, the FBI has grown into the giant it is now, and ironically, the Legislature never authorized their expansion. Everything was done administratively by the AG. Where does it say in the Constitution that a federal employee has the authority to create law, create a police authority, or to expand a current one?

Do you see how our government has circumvented the restrictions placed upon them by the Constitution, and manipulated the American people?

We the People of the United States of America

24
Catastrophes, Calamaties & Disasters

Every catastrophe, calamity or disaster has been planned and financed by our so-called public representatives; with an ulterior motive in mind. The creation of Homeland Security was created in this same way. A Terrorist attack was staged by hired men having connections to the Middle East.

I'm not going to go into the conspiracy, other than to say that President Bush and the FBI were as guilty as the men who high-jacked the commercial airplanes.

The director of the FBI confessed his Agency's involvement to Congress, under Presidential Order. He was relieved of his position, and Congress took no action against President Bush. And the media did not report any of this to the American people.

"911 WAS AN INSIDE JOB."

Treason charges have been filed against President Bush, Vice-President Cheney and the FBI, by a two star General from the Pentagon. No action has been taken and nothing was ever reported to the American public, upon orders of President Obama. This was just another government catastrophe designed to make you (the public) beg the government to come to your aid and protect you.

Each time one of these catastrophes is staged our representatives steal more of our liberty and freedom from us.

Government has eroded our rights. We've been lied to directly and indirectly, and told to believe something other than the truth. The correct term for this is: "Propaganda".

25
The Secret North American Alliance

During the Bush Administration, a Treaty called the North American Alliance was negotiated and signed, but the content of the Treaty was not reported to the American public. The Treaty guarantees that the boundary lines dividing Mexico, the United States and Canada will dissolve and become one country, to be called North America, upon the installation of the Government of the New World Order.

The currency for North America is being manufactured by the United States Mint. They are gold coins called AMEROS. There are pictures of these coins being minted, that were taken by an employee and smuggled out.

Everything in your life has been controlled from birth, and you are still being controlled. The free-thinkers of the world have either been murdered, or institutionalized in asylums. Freethinkers are a detriment to the Masters and their Agents. They have the potential to become Martyrs, especially if the populace begins to pay attention to what the free-thinkers have to say or teach.

Look at what happened to Jesus; John Kennedy; Bobby Kennedy; John Kennedy, Jr., and Martin Luther King, Jr. If you believe John Kennedy, Jr.'s was an accidental death, then you probably believe that 911 was not an inside job; that the attack on the twin towers was a real Terrorist attack.

Contrary to popular belief, nothing has changed since Jesus's day. If Jesus were alive today, he would be deemed a Terrorist and locked up in an asylum, and be slowly poisoned to death through the use of drug combinations designed to slowly take away life instead of to heal.

As long as free-thinkers profess their thoughts, they will be institutionalized until death. Society will be told that these men are dangerous and they will be classified as Terrorists.

26
The One World Government To Come

The entire World is a "Slave Plantation" and is set up under this same principle by the Masters, "the high contracting powers," who have been identified in certain International Treaties as the Pope/Vatican, the United Nations, the King/Queen of England or United Kingdom, and principals of the International Monetary Fund.

The coming of a "One World Government," which public representatives and the media have been talking about, actually began in 1790 with the passage of the Articles of Confederation. These Articles and the principles therein, were first suggested in the Magna Carta and later became the foundation of the U.S. Constitution, but "they are not for you."

The Capitol City of the World has been identified as New York City, according to the United States Code. The United Nations with the blessings of the Vatican, keeps the World divided and in flux, under the principle of "Divide and Conquer," and all religious orders within the United States are instructed to keep us docile and passive like sheep. People, populations, economies, religions and political agendas of every country on earth are manipulated by the Masters, which keep each Country in an euphoric flux against the other.

We are presently living under the Babylonian Talmud, which was introduced to England in 1066, and has been enforced by the Pope, various Kings, and every religious Order since. This Babylonian Talmud represents total and relentless mind control, in that people are taught to believe in fictions, things that do not exist.

Private International Law is now Commercial Law, which only deals in fictions; fictions called 'persons', 'money', 'politics', 'governments' and 'authority.'

The Uniform Commercial Code, known as the Law of Merchants, which is 6000 years old, was derived from ancient Babylon and is now Private International Law. (See: The Uniform Commercial Code, section 1-201).

P.S. Human rights do not exist in fictions.

27
How It All Came About

Prior to 1066, many of the Kings subjects (Lords and Dukes) held allodial deeds of title to land, which are land grants from the King, or past Kings, which prevented the present King or his agents from taxing, trespassing or enforcing his will upon those subjects.

Land protected by an allodial deed, and improved by a home, made the subjects, Sovereigns in their own right, and the kings of their castles. In 1066, William the Conqueror defeated England and stole the Kings Title, his lands and the lands belonging to his subjects.

From William I (1066) to King John (1199), England found itself in dire straights because it was bankrupt. During this span of time, parishioners routinely passed their land on to their family or to the church without the Kings permission. So the King invoked the ancient, "Law of Mortmain," also known as "the dead man's hand," which is our modern day probate law.

The Pope and the Vatican objected to the "Law of Mortmain" because the King owed the Vatican a lot of gold he had borrowed and this law now prevented the church from receiving gifts of land. In 1208, England was placed under Papal interdiction (prohibition) and King John was excommunicated from the Church. King John was ignorant of the teachings of the Bible and was made to believe, by Pope Innocent III, that the Pontiff was the "Vicar of Christ;" the ultimate owner of everything on earth, and the only one who could grant the King absolution for his sins; providing the

King make a suitable gesture of repentance to the Pope and the Holy Roman Church.

The word "VICAR" is defined in Webster's 1828 English Dictionary, to mean, "A person deputized or authorized to perform the function of another, a substitute in office," and thereafter, all of the Popes, since Pope Innocent III, pretend to be Jesus Christ on earth.

In his attempt to regain his stature, King John offered the Pope and the Holy Roman Church his Kingdom, plus 1000 gold marks each year, as payment of a lease on the land, and he accepted the Pope's appointed representative (appointed ruler) and swore submission and loyalty to Pope Innocent III and the Holy Roman Church.

In 1213, a Treaty was entered into between the King and the Pope. The Treaty made the King a tenant of his former Kingdom, and a trustee to the Pope and the Holy Roman Church. The King's ancestors were later appointed Treasurer of the Vatican Bank and continue to serve in that capacity to date.

See the Treaty of 1213; and the Papal Bulls of 1455 to 1492; and *Selected Letters of Pope Innocent III concerning England from 1198 - 1216,* Thomas Nelson and Sons, Ltd. 1956.

In 1215, the Barons of England reacted to the loss of their rights and privileges they once enjoyed before the 1213 Treaty, and so they revolted against King John and stormed the castle. Under the threat of death, they forced him to sign a document that recognized their stature and spelled out their individual rights. The document was named the Magna Carta (meaning Great Charta).

When Pope Innocent III was informed by King John about the Barons' revolt and the Magna Carta; the Pope condemned the document and declared it null and void.

In his written declaration to the Barons, the Pope stated that, "The Declaration of Human Rights embodied in the Magna Carta violated the tenets of the Church."

Imagine that — a Church that does not believe in human rights — but has a prohibition against abortion. I believe that is called, an Oxymoron.

(Ibid; *Selected Letters of Pope Innocent III concerning England 1198 - 1216,* Thomas Nelson and Sons, Ltd. 1956).

28
Two Treaties Of Note

The Treaty of 1783, known as the Treaty of Peace, signed in Paris, France, subsequent to the Revolutionary War; was between King George, the Holy Roman Church, and the representatives of the Corporate United States.

The opening statement is written in Olde English and when interpreted means: "The King claims that the Pope is the Vicar of Christ and that God gave the King the power to declare that no man can ever own property because it goes against the tenets of his Church, the Vatican/The Holy Roman Church, and because he is the Elector of the Holy Roman Empire." This is why no person or company can ever own real estate in America; and the Founding Fathers agreed to that Declaration.

The Treaty of Verona, which took place on November 22, 1822, was another Treaty between the King of England, the Pope, and the "high contracting powers" of the World, exemplifies the power that the Pope and the Vatican wield in the World, and magnifies their interest in the Republic of the United States. It also explains what has happened to us in America.

The Treaty of Verona . . .

Article I declares that the "high contracting powers" (the Masters) agree and decree that all representative forms of government and governments that recognize the individual sovereignty of ordinary people, are incompatible with "divine right", and all agree to use all of their efforts to bring an end to such governments wherever they may be found or exist. (Isn't the United States supposed to be a representative form of government which recognizes individual sovereignty? At least that's what the Declaration of Independence promised).

Article 2 declares that the "high contracting powers" agreed and decreed that freedom of the press is a detriment to their existence, and all promised to adopt measures to suppress the press in all of Europe.

If Americans want to know what is happening in the United States they need to tune into the Foreign News Service, because the American Press has been suppressed beyond belief, ever since the Nixon administration and the Watergate scandal.

America's Press, however, will talk badly about other countries, and the Foreign Press reciprocates the favor. Do you remember our earlier comment about, "Divide and Conquer?" If you want to know what is happening in America, you need to watch and listen to the Foreign Press.

Article 3 declares that, because religion contributes powerfully to keep the people in a state of passive obedience, all of the "high contracting powers" agree to take measures to ensure its continuation. A written accolade was directed to the Pope for his efforts to create and continue those measures.

An example of the measures they are speaking of involves the King James Bible.

29
The King James Version Of The Bible

The King James Version of the Bible was written by the King under the guidance of Pope Innocent III. The same King who was convinced by the Pope that the Pope was God's representative on earth. This collaboration was kept secret to conceal the truth of their manipulation of the Prophets' written word.

Some people even claim that, if you can locate an ancient manuscript of the Bible that predates the King James Version, you will discover that it was written in the ancient text that Jesus said: *"...forgive them not; for they know what they do."*

Whereas, it is written in the King James Version that Jesus said: *"...forgive them; for they know not what they do."* The King James interpretation represents a passive version in keeping with the purpose mentioned in the Treaty of Verona, in Article 3.

Nevertheless . . .

"It is the Spirit that quickeneth; the flesh profiteth nothing: the words that I (Jesus) *speak unto you, they are spirit, and they are life".*
— John 6:32.

The King James Version of the Bible is the most popular version today and is presented to the masses by all government controlled Christian religions.

A Different Point Of View

Passive obedience, however, is not taught or practiced in the Muslim religion.

What was the lie our government used to explain the involvement of the armed forces of the United States and England in the Middle East? I recall Muslim leaders' accusation and claim that this was a "Jihad" — a holy war against them — and that our so-called leaders denied the allegation. When the American people were later questioned by the media, they too responded with disdain and disbelief.

Is it any wonder that there are now Muslim paramilitary camps being formed on American soil? When our government officials were questioned as to why they permit these paramilitary camps to exist, their response is that the U.S. Constitution protects their right to exist.

This is the same Constitution that we are not a party too; that our government officials have circumvented, and that fails to protect We the People's rights.

30
Power Centers Of The World

Written by Several sources:

The Vatican rules over approximately 2 billion of the world's 6.1 billion people. The colossal wealth of the Vatican includes enormous investments with the Rothschilds in Britain, France, and the USA, and with giant oil and weapons corporations like General Electric and Shell Oil. The Vatican's solid gold bullion, worth billions, is stored with the Rothschild controlled Bank of England and the United States Federal Reserve Bank.

The Catholic Church is the biggest financial power, wealth accumulator, and property owner in existence. Possessing more material wealth than any bank, corporation, giant trust, or government, anywhere on the globe. The Pope, who is the visible ruler of this colossal global wealth is one of the richest men on Earth. While two-thirds of the world earns less than two dollars a day, and one-fifth of the world is under fed or starving to death, the Vatican hordes the world's wealth, profits from it on the stock market, and at the same time preaches about "giving."

Like Vatican City, London's Inner city is also a privately owned corporation, or city state, located right in the heart of Greater London. It became a sovereign state in 1694 when King William III of Orange privatized the Bank of England turning it over to the bankers. By 1812 Nathan Rothschild had crashed the English stock market and scammed control of the Bank of England. Today the City (state) of London is the world's financial power centre and the wealthiest square mile on the face of the Earth. It houses the Rothschild controlled Bank of England, Lloyd's of London, the London Stock Exchange, all British Banks, the branch offices of 385 foreign banks, and 70 US banks. It has its own courts, its own laws, its own flag, and its own police force. It's not part of Greater London, England, or the British Commonwealth, and pays no taxes. The City of London houses Fleet Street's newspaper and publishing monopolies. It is also the headquarters for worldwide English Freemasonry, and headquarters for the worldwide money cartel know as the "Crown."

Contrary to popular belief the Crown is not the Royal Family or the British Monarch. The Crown is the private corporate City of London. It has a council of twelve members who rule the corporation under a mayor called the Lord Mayor. The Lord Mayor and his twelve member council serve as prophecies, or representatives, who sit in for thirteen of the world's wealthiest, most powerful banking families.

This ring of thirteen ruling families includes the Rothschild family, the Warburg family, the Oppenheimer family, and the Schiff family. These families and their descendants run the Crown Corporation of London. The Crown Corporation holds the title to worldwide Crown Land, in Crown Colonies like Canada, Australia, and New Zealand. The British Parliament and the British Prime Minister serve as a public front for these ruling Crown Families.

Like the city states of London and the Vatican, a third city state was officially created in 1790 as the first Act of the Constitution for America. That city state is called the District of Columbia and is located on ten square miles of land in the State of Maryland. The District of Columbia flies its own flag and has its own independent Constitution.

Although geographically separate, the city states of London, the Vatican City, and the District of Columbia, are one interlocking empire called the Empire of the City (*meaning Columbia*).

The flag of the District of Columbia has two horizontal red bars on a field of white, making three horizontal white bars, with three red stars evenly space on the top white bar — signifying Military Control (*from Washington DC*); Financial Control (*from the Inner City of London*); and Religious Control (*from Vatican City*).

The Constitution for the District of Columbia operates under a tyrannical Roman law known as Lex Fori which bares no resemblance to the original U.S. Constitution.

When Congress passed the Act of 1871 it created a separate corporate government for the District of Columbia. This treasonous act allowed the District of Columbia to operate as a corporation outside the original U.S. Constitution and outside of the best interest of American citizens.

A sobering study of the signed Treaties and Charters, between Britain and the United States, exposes a shocking truth that the United States has always been and still is a British Crown Colony. King James I was famous, not for just changing the Bible into the King James Version, but for signing the First Charter of Virginia in 1606. That Charter granted America's British Forefathers a license to settle and colonize America. The Charter also guarantees that future Kings and Queens of England would have sovereign authority over all the citizens and colonized land in America that was stolen from the Indians.

Although King George III of England gave up most of his claims over the American Colonies, he kept his right to continue receiving payment for his business venture of colonizing America. If America had really won the war of independence they would never have agreed to pay debts and reparations to the King of England via Jay's Treaty.

America's blood soaked War of Independence against the British, bankrupted America and turned its citizens into permanent debt slaves of the King. In the War of 1812 the British torched and burned the White House to the ground, and all US government buildings, and destroyed the ratification records of the US Constitution.

In 1604, a Corporation called the Virginia Company was formed in anticipation of the imminent influx of white Europeans, mostly British at first, into the North American continent. Its main stockholder was King James I, and the original charter for the company was completed by April 10th 1606.

The Virginia Company owned most of the land of what we now call the USA. The Virginia Company (The British Crown and the bloodline families) had rights to 50%, yes 50%, of all gold and silver mined on its lands, plus percentages of other minerals and raw materials, and 5% of all profits from other ventures. The lands of the Virginia Company were granted to the colonies under a Deed of Trust (on lease) and therefore they could not claim ownership of the land. They could pass on *the perpetual use* of the land to their heirs or sell *the perpetual use* of the land, but they could never own it. Ownership is retained by the British Crown.

The original American Constitution reads: **"The Constitution FOR the united States of America"** which ended with the original 13th Amendment; destroyed in the war of 1812. The Post Bellam version reads: **"The Constitution OF the United States of America"**. (emphasis mine).

When Americans agree to have a Social Security number, the citizens of the united states surrender their sovereignty and agree to become franchises of the United States (The Virginia Company of the British Crown).

Everything in the "United States" is for sale: roads, bridges, schools, hospitals, water, prisons, airports etc. (Executive Order 12803)

The "Crown" that owns Virginia (USA) is the administrative Corporation of the City of London, a State independent of Great Britain and wholly owned by the Pontiff of Rome. Since 1213, the Monarchs of England have been puppet Monarchs under the Pontifex Maximus of the Holy Roman Empire, a corporate body over which the Pontiff of Rome is CEO. Since 1300, when the Crown of Great Britain (England) was made a sub-corporation of the Crown of the City of London, the Monarchs of England, as CEO of the Crown of Great Britain have been agents for the Crown of the City. Thus, the *real* Crown was obfuscated from the eyes of the "colonials". But, anyone who cared to look, and reason, could have seen this scheme even in the late 1700's A.D.

The 'common law' of England, since the incorporation of the British Crown, circa 1300 A.D., has been Roman Municipal Law, a type of Roman civil law designed to rule over debtor States. The Anglo-Saxon common law, which used only "God's Law", ceased to exist with the implementation of the feudal system where all people were subjects of the corporate Crown, and after the Pope's Papal Bull, Unam Sanctam 1302, where he declared: "Furthermore, we declare, we proclaim, we define that it is absolutely necessary for salvation that every human creature be subject to the Roman Pontiff." ("subject" means slave, as does "citizen" and "freeman").

Roman Law uses the "law of the sea" because all human institutions in the Roman system are make-believe ships at sea (incorporated bodies, or vessels).

The "all caps" spelling does not make the "legal identity name" into the strawman that it represents. The all caps signifies that the strawman name carries with its use the status of slave, pledged as Chattel in the Bankruptcy of the State.

*City of London + City of Vatican + City of Columbia are the 3 independent city states within states which comprise the Empire of the City. The first city state is financial control over the earth's economy, the second city state is religious control over the earth's religions and the third city state is military control over the earth itself. Together they make the very unholy trinity which forms the Egyptian pyramid that we can see on the back of the privately owned federal reserve note that is used as the American dollar to maintain the colony in debt under the Queen.

Many people realize that this mystifying situation, in which an alleged democratic and self-governing nation is actually controlled against the will of the people, is a clear indication that there must be a very powerful and well-financed occult organization which plans and directs world affairs, and for lack of a more specific identification the suspected secret organization is popularly referred to as the International Financiers, Banker Cartel or "The Crown corporation".

31
How We Americans Were Enslaved

We are political prisoners of the "shadow government" that now controls the USA. The American system is but a "slip" off the same plant: the British limited Monarchy.

Why do the courts refuse to admit certain arguments and citings of the United States Constitution and find some people in contempt of court if they persist in doing so? Why is there so little justice in our court system today? Our problem is that we have been fighting the wrong system — playing the wrong ball game.

We are not in Common Law under the Constitution. We're not in Equity under the Constitution. We're in Maritime Law, the Law of Commerce, the Law of Admiralty.

Admiralty Law encompasses all controversies arising out of acts done upon or relating to the sea and questions of prize. Prize is that law dealing with war and the spoils of war — such as capture of ships, goods, materials, property — both real and personal, etc.

Maritime Law is that system of law that relates to Commerce and Navigation on the high seas. Because of this, you don't have to be on a ship in the middle of the sea to be under Admiralty Jurisdiction. This jurisdiction can attach merely because the subject matter falls within the scope of Maritime Law. Negotiable bills, notes, checks, and credits are within the scope of Maritime Law.

Admiralty Law grew and developed from the harsh realities and expedient measures required to survive at sea. Because of its genesis, it contains a harsh set of rules and procedures wherein there is no right to trial by jury, no right to privacy, etc. In other words, there are **no rights** under Admiralty jurisdiction — only **privileges** granted by the Captain of the ship, on the maritime voyage.

In this jurisdiction there is no such thing as a right to not be compelled to testify against oneself in a criminal case — the Captain of the ship can, *however if he wishes,* grant you the **privilege** against self-incrimination. There's no such thing as a right to use your property on the public highways — but the Captain may grant you the **privilege** to do so if he chooses. There is no such thing as a right to operate your own business — only a **privilege** allowed as long as you perform according to the Captain's regulations.

Back at the time just prior to the Revolution — when our Colonies were festering and threatening revolt against the King — when we had the Common Law of the Colonies — the King's men came over to collect their taxes. They didn't apply the Common Law, they applied Admiralty Law — arrested people, held Star Chamber proceedings, and denied us the common law rights of Englishmen.

This, more than any one thing (sure, taxation without representation was part of it) was a denial of our Common Law rights, by putting us under Admiralty Law wherein the Chancellor was the King. His agents deprived us of jury trials, put us on ships, sent us down to ports in the British West Indies where many died of fever in the holds of ships and very few returned. This was one of the main reasons for the Revolution of 1776.

Historically, the common law had come from the Anglo-Saxon common law in England. It existed and ruled England prior to the reign of William the Conqueror [1066] when the Normans conquered Anglo-Saxon England.

The common law was based on the Golden Rule in its negative form: the Rule of Civil Justice that in the negative form reads: **"Do *not* unto others, as you would *not* have others do unto you"** — the Rule of *Civil Justice*. (The *positive* form deals with *Social Justice*.)

Where did this law come from — this Anglo-Saxon Common Law? Did it come from Christianity's introduction to England? Apparently not. It is on record in the Vatican that early Christian missionaries reported that the people of Northern Germany *"already have the law."* It is suspected that early Hebrew traders in tin taught these people the law, many years before Christ.

So, the English people had this simple and pure Common Law of human rights and property rights. But there also existed along side of it, even in those days, the law of commerce, *Commercial Law* — which is Maritime Law.

The earliest record we have of Maritime Law is in the Isle of Rhodes (900 B. C.) Then there's the Laws of Oleron, Laws of the Hanseatic League, Maritime Law which was part and parcel of their civil law.

Maritime Law is the law of commerce.

The common law was the law that had to do with the land, and the people of the land.

William the Conqueror subjugated all the Saxons to his rule, except London Town. The merchants controlled the city, and their walls held off the invaders. The merchants provisioned the city by ships, and William's soldiers failed to prevail. Finally, acknowledging that he could not take the City by force, William resorted to compromise. The merchants demanded the **"Lex Mercantoria"** (Maritime Law), **which was granted and remains to this day.** The Inner City of London has its special law — **the Merchant's Law** — the law of the City of London.

Protection of their shipping industry was one of the main reasons for the resistance by the merchants of London.

The Saxon Common Law had no provision for **fictitious persons (*companies*)** or **limited liability.** It recognized only **natural persons** and **full liability**.

Roman Civil Law is a derivative of Maritime Law and is the basis of Civil Law in most European Countries. The identifying features of Roman Common Law are the usage of ***precedent*** and ***judgement by magistrate(s)*** in courts of **Summary Jurisdiction.**

At Runnymede, in 1215, the Barons of England forced King John to sign the Magna Carta, one of several documents that establish the fundamental rights of the English people to this day, the others being the revision of the Magna Carta in 1225, the Petition of Rights of 1628, and the Bill of Rights of 1689.

The Magna Carta was implemented to *prohibit* the use of the Summary Jurisdiction of Roman or Admiralty Law to authorize taxation and the seizure of property without due process of law nor just compensation.

The colonists were well schooled in the common law and were well aware of the wrongs that the King and the Parliament were committing against them. This eventually forced them to rebel.

The common law that we had in our land is parallel to another ancient law. When our Founding Fathers set up a **Declaratory Trust** (Declaration of Independence), Jefferson listed 18 grievances. In each one of these grievances he showed how **we were being denied our rights as free-born Englishmen**.

Jefferson appealed to the nations of the world, that the acts being committed against the colonists were acts committed against the Law of Nations. So his **Declaratory Trust** (Declaration of Independence) **became a Public Trust: an ordinance** *within* **the Law of Nations.** The Founding Fathers knew that they would have to fight to win the Independence that they just so courageously had declared.

After the British surrendered at Yorktown, the Articles of Confederation period followed. Our Founding Fathers integrated the Constitution into this Public Trust, which became the mechanism to provide for us hopes and aspirations.

In the Constitution are principles, but not necessarily those found in the Declaration of Independence.

Some of the writers of the Constitution were a little too restrictive. It was generally conceded, for instance, that the people had *the right to bear arms,* but they also knew that if we ever were placed or allowed ourselves to be brought under Maritime Admiralty Law, *with regard to our persons and property,* we would have dire need of a guarantee of our rights — thus, **the 10 Articles of the Bill of Rights** were written to supplement and reinforce the Constitution.

The Maritime Admiralty jurisdiction is defined in Article III, Section 2, of the Constitution. (to follow)

We have been tricked out of our Common Law rights; into the Admiralty courts.

Equity and Admiralty have been corrupted.

The Federal Government has made it practically impossible for us to receive our constitutional rights; our substantive rights in the Constitution.

How?

The Admiralty/Maritime jurisdiction of Congress is defined in U.S. Constitution (1787) Article I, Section 8:

8.1. The Congress shall have the power to ... collect taxes, duties, imposts and excises, to pay the debts ... of the United States:

8.2. To borrow money on the credit of the United States;

8.3. To regulate Commerce with foreign nations, and among the several States, and with the Indian Tribes;

8.4. To establish a uniform rule of naturalization, and uniform laws on the subject of bankruptcies...

8.10. To define and punish piracies and felonies committed on the high seas, and offenses against the Law of Nations;

8.11. To declare war, grant letters of marque and reprisal, and make rules concerning captures on land and water;

8.12. To raise and support armies...

8.13. To provide and maintain a navy;

8.14. To make rules for...land and naval forces;

8.15. To provide for calling forth the militia...

8.16. To provide for organizing, arming, and disciplining the militia...

The 11 powers listed above are all within the jurisdiction

of Admiralty/Maritime Law, and encompass all but 7 of the 18 powers granted to Congress.

The Admiralty/Maritime jurisdiction <u>of the Supreme Court</u> is defined in U.S. Constitution (1787) Article III, Section 2:

> 2.1. The judicial power shall extend to all cases in law and equity, arising under this Constitution, the laws of the United States, and treaties made, or which shall be made, under their authority; to all cases affecting ambassadors, other public minister and consuls; to *all cases of admiralty and maritime jurisdiction;* to controversies ...

The full scope and meaning of Article III, Section 2, was addressed by Justice Story in *De Lovio v. Boit* in 1815:

> *"What is the true interpretation of the clause, all cases of admiralty and maritime jurisdiction?"*

If we examine the etymology, or received use of the words *"admiralty"* and *"maritime jurisdiction,"* we shall find, that they include **jurisdiction of all things done upon and relating to the sea,** or in other words, all transactions and proceedings relative to commerce and navigation and to damages or injuries upon the sea.

In all the great maritime nations of Europe, the same "admiralty jurisdiction" is uniformly applied to the courts exercising jurisdiction over maritime contract and concerns. We shall find the terms just as familiarly known among the jurists of Scotland, France, Holland and Spain, as of England, and applied to their own courts, possessing substantially the same jurisdiction as the English Admiralty in the reign of Edward the Third.

"The clause, however, of the constitution not only confers admiralty jurisdiction, but the word 'maritime' is super-added, seemingly ex-industria, to remove every latent doubt. Cases of maritime jurisdiction must include all maritime contracts, injuries, and torts, which are in the understanding of common law as well as of admiralty..."

In U.S. Constitution (1787) Article VI it is stated:

6.1. "All debts contracted and engagements entered into, before the adoption of this Constitution, shall be valid against the United States under this Constitution, as under the Confederation.

6.2. "This Constitution, and the laws of the United States which shall be made in pursuance thereof; and all treaties made, or which shall be made, under the authority of the United States, shall be the supreme law of the land; and the judges in every State shall be bound thereby, any thing in the constitution or laws of any State to the contrary notwithstanding."

Clearly, the Admiralty/Maritime jurisdiction that was granted to Congress and the Judiciary is very extensive and broad.

32
How The Law Was Lost

Adapted from *The Tyranny of Good Intentions,* by Paul Craig Roberts and Lawrence M. Stratton (2000).

Legal Philosophers have approached the study of jurisprudence from different schools of thought.

For example: natural law versus positive law; legal realism versus legal formalism; or judicial activism versus original intent.

The real question is whether law protects the people from government, or enables government to lord it over the people. The control that democracy gave the people over government made the people feel safe — free from the unaccountable power of an earthly lord.

The questions are: "Since the government is ours and accountable to us, what is the purpose of a legal system that protects us from a power that we control? Does not the emphasis on individual rights prevent us from using our government to achieve the greatest benefit for the greatest number of people?"

The 18th Century British philosopher Jeremy Bentham answered in the affirmative. "Yes...the emphasis on individual rights prevents us from using our government to achieve the greatest benefit for the greatest number of people."

This new concept began a legal revolution in which the people's rights would again become subservient to the greater interests of the state.

Bentham's concept of law, as a tool for socially engineering a higher level of happiness, contrasted sharply with William Blackstone's concept of law, as the people's shield from the tyranny of a centralized government's control.

Most Americans think of law as a long list of deeds that the government prohibits them to do.

What Blackstone means by law, is a handful of prohibitions **on** government, not prohibitions **from** government — that law is a handful of principles that prevent the government from using the legal system as an instrument of oppression — the requirement that law serves justice, not government.

The government defines justice in all other systems of law, thus leaving the people vulnerable to government persecution and control.

Blackstone praised England's "laws and liberties" as "the birthright and noblest inheritance of mankind." Perhaps no other book — except the Bible — has played so great a role as Blackstone's *Commentaries on the Laws of England* — a colonial best-seller, nearly matching England's sales.

The colonists' Declaration of Independence essentially affirmed their rights as Englishmen that they felt King George III had trampled under foot. When members of the Continental Congress signed the Declaration of Independence (July 4, 1776) pledging to each other, their Lives, their Fortunes, and their sacred Honor, they were infused with the confidence that they stood with both feet planted in English law, more so than King George.

That same year, Blackstone's concept of law as a shield was attacked by an anonymous tract, written by Jeremy Bentham himself.

Bentham lamented the erection of new legal barriers that blocked government from doing communal good works. Bentham wanted to remake the world. He saw English law as a barrier to Liberty, and Blackstonian law as a barrier to those who want to remake society and the world, like himself.

Bentham found *'liberal'* and *'liberty'* to be mischievous words. The real issues, he declared, were happiness and security. What good is liberty, he asked, if the absence of governmental action means that people are not happy and feel insecure. His pamphlet *"Fragment on Government"* saw liberty as the freedom of government from restraint, not the freedom of the people from government.

Bentham saw law as government's instrument for doing good, because, he taught, the purpose of both government and law is to promote the "greatest happiness for the greatest number" — that social engineering to enhance the greater good takes precedence of the Englishman's rights.

Bentham's heaven was a Gulag.

It's easy to impute good motives and draw up lists of good things that government could do if only there were no chains on its powers. But this could make sense only to a people who had tied government down, so it could do them no harm.

Blackstone's theme of patience, and the importance of treading slowly, was lost on **Bentham's** impatience.

Blackstone's concept of law gave us Englishman's rights. **Bentham's** concept undermined those rights.

For **Blackstone,** law was the people's shield. For **Bentham,** it was permissible for the government to trample upon the individual in the name of a "greater good."

Blackstone respected property as an "absolute right, inherent in every Englishman." **Bentham** thought private property was merely a legally dispensable creation of the government.

Blackstone thought law was grounded in the values and traditions of the people. **Bentham** thought law could be scientifically remade by the government in pursuit of "the greatest happiness for the greatest number."

Blackstone revered juries and reviled the Court of Star Chamber, which Parliament had abolished in 1641 for its tyranny. **Bentham** hated juries and praised the Court of Star Chamber for its efficacy in securing convictions.

For **Blackstone**, law was a shield held by the people against government. For **Bentham**, law was a sword wielded by government over the people for their own good.

Bentham believed in the wisdom and perfectibility of public administrators. **Blackstone** feared the government's "evil and pernicious counselors" and defended constitutional diffusions of power.

Blackstone was conscous of human fallibility. **Bentham** trumpeted the limitless powers of reason.

Blackstone was an incrementalist. **Bentham** was a radical.

Bentham died on June 6, 1832 but his legacy has continued.

The history of English legal reform in the 19th century is the story of the shadow cast by one man: Bentham.

It did not take long for **Bentham's shadow** to reach America, where his concepts would ultimately dissect the rights of Englishmen out of United States law.

There was never a radical frontal assault that over threw these rights. Rather, it has been a piecemeal and incomplete process.

We can no longer take for granted that we will be afforded the protections provided by the Englishman's rights.

33
The Robbers Of Today

In the Dark Ages, government officials used their police powers to enrich themselves by seizing travelers of means who passed through their jurisdiction and imprisoning them until their ransom was paid.

Their counterparts in the United States today bypass the hostage taking and simply seize the property outright.

Most Americans are unaware of the police state that has crept up upon us from many directions.

The DEA (Drug Enforcement Administration) maintains confiscation squads at major airports and has turned airline and airport employees into informers by awarding them 10 percent of confiscated assets.

The DEA also maintains surveillance operations in hotels.

Innocent people can lose their property for no other reason than reporting possible criminal activity to the police.

The secret of law enforcement officers' success is that they don't have to bring charges against the owners of the property that they seize. The Comprehensive Forfeiture Act, passed in 1984, allows police to confiscate property on "probable cause" — the same minimum standard needed by police to justify a search.

The law places the burden on the owner to prove that his confiscated property was not used to facilitate a crime.

The government can confiscate a person's property without convicting him or even charging him with a crime. Moreover, the property can remain forfeited even if the accused is acquitted of charges.

The asset forfeiture laws have given birth to the American police state. The law that protects us from tyrannical police actions has been lost to good intentions.

Due process; the presumption of innocence until proven guilty; the right to counsel; the prohibition against punishment based on presumption; and the ban on retroactive law, have all fallen to good intentions.

Good intentions have changed law from a shield for the innocent to a weapon used by police in a police state.

Americans are as yet unaware of their plight because the U.S. population is large relative to the number of police and their prosecutorial actions. If the confiscations were universal the American people would rise up against the new Robbers of today.

The random nature of the abuses of the police state is eating away at our rights and slowly acclimating Americans to tyranny.

Justice ceases to exist.

When justice breaks down the result is oppression.

Example

At 8:36 A.M. on October 2, 1992, thirty armed members of an "entry team" led by Los Angeles deputy sheriffs John Cater and Gary Spencer broke down the front door of multimillionaire Donald Scott's home on his 200 acre oceanfront estate in Malibu, California, and shot him dead. Mr. Scott was not on the FBI's most wanted list. He was holding no one hostage. He had committed no crime, and he had defied no summons. He was shot dead because Mr. Spencer had targeted Scott's estate for asset forfeiture on trumped-up charges. The conspiracy to deprive Scott of his property, that ended with depriving him of his life, went unpunished.

The presumptive seizure of property permitted by the Comprehensive Forfeiture Act of 1984 permits property to be seized on "probable cause" and inflicts punishment without proof. It reverses the presumption of innocence that is the basis of our criminal justice system and contravenes another of the fundamental rights of mankind — no crime without intent. Asset forfeiture has created a great temptation for state and local police departments to target assets rather than criminal activity.

34
Untoward Change

America's reputation as "the Land of the Free" — in the Anglo-Saxon legal and political tradition — has nearly been lost. Americans are losing the accountability of law that ensures that the state is their servant rather than their master.

We Americans are losing the protections of law, because we have forgotten why these safe-guards are important.

As a "former" British Colony, Americans inherited the English legal system in which law developed as a means of pursuing justice and finding the truth. The U.S. Legal System was based on English precedent.

In recent times, however, reverence for our legal system has been replaced by fear, dissatisfaction, and distrust.

The primary obligation of each generation is to pass on, undiminished, the institutions of liberty and the basic rights of mankind — the legal principles that prevent law from being used as a weapon of the State against the people.

True freedom in America is based upon the restraint of government power by law that is accountable to the people. Earning our freedom anew requires that we believe in the accountability of law.

We in America are gradually undergoing a transformation of our government into an administrative State similar to that achieved overnight in Germany, in 1933, with the passage of the Enabling Act of the German Reichstag that transferred law making power from the legislative to the executive branch of the National Socialist State.

The Enabling Act gave dictatorial power to Adolf Hitler and almost facilitated the Nazi take over of the world.

Self-rule ceases to exist when elected representatives no longer make the law.

Eventually, power that is unrestrained becomes unlimited power based directly on force where even the powerful elite are defenseless against the law when it is used as a weapon.

Almost all of our legal protections, which took centuries to achieve, have, on the threshold of the 21st Century, now been lost.

35
The Non-delegation Doctrine

Law is the set of principles that protects citizens from tyranny: Where there can be no crime without intent; no retroactive liability; no self-incrimination; no invasions of the attorney-client privilege; no infringements of a vigorous and vocal defense; where a person's property is respected as an extension of himself; and where prosecutors exercise sober discretion.

Each of these protections, which took centuries to evolve, has taken a ferocious beating during the 20th century in America. Today even wealthy and prominent Americans are less secure in law than were unemployed English coal miners in the 1930s.

To ensure the permanence of these safeguards that make law a protector of people rather than a weapon to be used against them, **the Founding Fathers made law accountable to the people.**

In the system they devised, people would never have to suffer from the imposition of unjust rules of conduct because the people themselves rather than governing elites would control the rules under which they agreed to live. **Representatives elected through the democratic process would be the sole makers of laws.** Law resides in the hearts of the people rather than the mouth of the king.

The Constitution's first seventy-seven words sum up this monitored design.

"We the People of the United States, in order to form a more perfect union, establish justice, insure domestic tranquility, provide for the common defense, promote the general welfare, and secure the blessings of liberty to ourselves and our posterity, do ordain and establish this Constitution for the United States of America. All legislative powers herein granted shall be vested in a Congress of the United States, which shall consist of a Senate and House of Representatives."

All legislative power — the exclusive authority to make, alter, amend, and repeal laws — is reposed within the U.S. Congress. **"We the People" delegated "all legislative powers" to the U.S. Congress, period.**

Legislative power must remain in the body where it is placed by the Constitution.

"We the People" vested "all legislative powers" to elected representatives, only. Congress cannot lawfully delegate the lawmaking power to anyone else, otherwise, self-rule is a farse.

This corollary is expressed in the Anglo-Saxon legal maxim *Delegata potestas non potest delega.* **A delegated power cannot itself be delegated.**

The purpose of this restriction on **delegation** is to maintain the accountability of lawmakers. **Delegation** allows Congress to avoid responsibility for the protections of the law. John Locke wrote that **the people cannot be bound by any laws except those that are made by their elected representatives.** When law enforcers are at the same time lawmakers, there can be no liberty. American authorities are and should be forced to remember their popular origins and the power from which they emanate.

The requirement in Article I of the U.S. Constitution that Congress make all laws has been ignored for the greater part of the 20th century and also today. It is as though the Constitution has been altogether abolished because people secure in the law lost sight of the reasons for their safety.

As in America today, The Great Depression instilled in a generation of Americans a fear of unemployment and an impecunious old age. A coterie of government activists pushed the **delegat**ion of legislative power from Congress to agencies of the Executive branch. Bills were written by the executive branch at an assembly line pace. There were instances when, without any member's having seen a word of the text, without anything more than the title being read, adoption would be at once automatically voted into law.

The mistaken monetary policy of the non-federal Federal Reserve, together with mistaken fiscal policy, created the confidence-shattering Great Depression which was used to destroy the historic achievement of **the non-delegation doctrine** that was enshrined in the Constitution as a bulwark against tyranny.

This resurrection of the conditions for tyranny has been thinly veiled by the doctrine of legislative branch oversight of the regulatory agencies.

Even those who favored railroad antitrust and banking legislation in the late 19th and early 20th centuries respected **the non-delegation doctrine** and attempted to draft statutes so that executive enforcement personnel could never become lawmakers.

The Court's resistance to legislative **delegation** was soon dissipated under pressure by President Franklin

Delano Roosevelt's court-packing initiative.

Although today the judiciary gives lip service to **the non-delegation doctrine,** jurists never find **delegations** to be unconstitutional. Today **non-delegation,** the achievement of a thousand-year struggle, is a dead legged constitutional principle.

As long as administrative agencies purport to follow an undefined "intelligent principle" in a statute — such as "promoting the public interest"; "fair and equitable prices"; "fighting excessive profits"; or "imminent hazards to public safety"; etc. — unelected bureaucrats have free rein to make unlawful unlegislated law.

Paid commentators routinely refer to **the non-delegation doctrine** as "moribund"; "enfeebled"; "lacking substance". They view legislative **delegation** to administrative agencies as the "legal expression" of post-New Deal government

As the administrative state was taking shape, only a learned few appreciated the dangers to personal liberty and private property accompanying legislative **delegation** to special agencies or Czars.

Prior to the New Deal, legislation tended to be specifically and tightly written in order to avoid delegating the law to executive branch enforcers.

The so-called virtue of expertise became the basis for the growth of the administrative state.

The Soviet State, with totally unaccountable law, was promising a New Man and a New Society. Italy had Benito Mussolini's cooperative State. New Dealers were not going to let America be left behind the tide of history. The massive **delegation** of power to President Roosevelt took place in the same year the German Reichstag delegated all its powers to Adolph Hitler. Upon hearing of the National Industrial Recovery Act, Mussolini remarked of Roosevelt, *"ecco un ditatore"* — behold the dictator.

Faith that men bred to politics are superior in governance to men bred to the facts is still the false claim of our time

The contending forces struggling to influence the shape of society focus on controlling the executive agencies and the federal courts. For example, four days prior to Ronald Reagan's inauguration in January 1981, the Carter administration issued two volumes of new regulations to advance agendas that the people themselves had just voted against.

Democracy has no friends. The administrative State grows irrespective of the political coloration of the White House and the Congress.

Today bureaucrats can define criminal offense on the spot by how they interpret the regulation that they write. This gives regulatory bureaucrats vast discretion in defining the law. This wde range of discretion is an example of **delegation** at its worst. The ability of bureaucrats to define the law dispenses with the hallowed principle of no crime without intent and no retroactive crimes.

The spontaneous creation of criminal offenses by bureaucratic interpretation has contributed to the destruction of prosecutorial restraint.

When the United States was founded, piracy, treason, and counterfeiting were the only federal crimes. Today there are more than 3,000 crimes that derive from statutes and 10,000 that have been created by often needless regulation.

We no longer have a constitutional order, a separation of power, self-rule, or a rule of law when the Supreme Court permits a federal bureaucrat to usurp powers explicitly prohibited in statutory law in order to make prohibited actions the law of the land. Little wonder that the Federal Communication Commission has usurped the power of the purse and imposed the telephone tax effective January 1998.

We the People have vanished. Our place has been taken over by "wise men" and anointed elites.

We are still faced with the pretense of congressional oversight and the scholasticism of the Administrative Procedure Act. This facade lacks the honesty of the Enabling Act passed by the German Richstag which delegated legislative power to Hitler's executive branch, and which reads as thusly:

"In addition to the procedure for the passage of legislation outlined in the Constitution, the Reich Cabinet is also authorized to enact Laws... The national laws enacted by the Reich Cabinet may deviate from the Constitution... The national laws enacted by the Reich Cabinet shall be prepared by the Chancellor (i.e. Chancellor Adolf Hitler) and published in the official gazette. They come into effect, unless otherwise specified, upon the day following their publication."

36
What Must Be Done

The real problem with the criminal justice system is the erosion of Englishman's rights, not only in law but in the consciousness and attitudes of police, prosecutors, lawyers, judges, and the general public itself.

It is more important for the prosecutor to obtain a conviction, usually with plea bargaining, than to obtain justice. The justice system serves careers, not truth, and when our rights get in the way of careers, it is our rights that are cast aside.

When billionaire Michael Milken and hotel queen Leona Helmsley were framed, celebrities did not rush to their cause. Milken and Helmsley were white and rich and obviously not victims of racist white justice. The presumption was that they must have been guilty. The supposition that only blacks and other minorities can be framed hinders any concerted effort to reform a justice system that has become tyrannical.

This tyranny spreads like cancer. What happens, for example, when corrupt prosecutors, who gain name recognition by using any means to capitalize on their fame, enter politics or prestigious law firms?

Their lack of ethics and their manipulative ways go with them. Politics becomes even dirtier. Law firms are shaken loose from time-honored principles as partners are pried loose from their ethics in order to compete in the new ways.

Bill Gates is possibly the richest person in the world. His company, Microsoft, is maybe the most valuable company.

In the parlance of this era, Gates and Microsoft are at the top of the "hegemonic order."

Most antitrust experts believed the case against Microsoft was without foundation but that harm would come in the future when Microsoft would begin acting like a monopolist. In other words, Microsoft was on trial for how it was allegedly going to act in the future.

Here in all its glory was the Jerry Bentham proactive approach of punishing crime before it was committed.

Microsoft was hauled into court because defeated competitors sought to regain through political campaign contributions and government lobbying what they had lost in the marketplace, thinking that Bill Gate's childlike personality would make him a poor witness.

Prosecutors supply the interpretations of events that people read in their newspapers and watch on TV.

When a man who is known to be very smart comes across as a poor witness, it creates the suspicion that he is lying or hiding the truth, when this is not so. This is especially the case when the substantive issues are over the heads of jurors, reporters, and the judge himself.

Success in using law as a weapon in full view of the public and legal profession, is a clear indication that our legal system has degenerated into tyranny.

The plight of American democracy is beyond the reach of legal reform alone. Our constitutional system and its precepts have lost the allegiance of American elites. Legislation is no solution when bureaucrats stand statutes — which are not true laws — on their heads, and the Supreme Court will not defend the Constitution, or Congress' own legislative and monitoring powers.

Without an intellectual rebirth of constitutionalism there is no hope for American democracy. Arbitrary power and the rule of the Constitution cannot both exist at the same time. They are antagonistic, incompatible forces. One or the other must of necessity perish whenever they are brought into conflict.

The fervent belief that government power is a force for good and must be set free and not restrained is the opposite of liberalism; it is progressivism instead. The New Deal conversion of liberalism into progressivism, by unrestraining power, unleashed evil and injustice.

Today Americans increasingly feel defenseless in the face of the government that they think they control. What was formerly a patriotic flag waving element of the population has been organizing itself into "tea parties" and private militias.

In 1995, in the Oklahoma City Bombing, a terrorist act was committed by Americans against the American Government. Numerous polls show a widespread distrust and alienation of "We the People" from our own government.

The attitudes of militarized federal law enforcement agencies toward the people of America show the same distrust. In 1995, Pennsylvania Avenue was close off around the White House, making it, as the symbol of the American Republic, similar to the walled Kremlin of the Soviets.

We see no hope for an intellectual rebirth that would let us reclaim our legal and political tradition of limited and restrained power. This cause for hope is the universal failure of government. The twentieth century's disasters were all based in high hopes placed on government power.

German National Socialism, Soviet and Chinese communism, French and African development planning, Asian industrial policy, and American New Dealism all failed.

The Benthamite commitment to government that has colored society and thinking about law — and the proselytizing power of the secular worship of government — must be now seen. The time is ripe for true liberalism to make a comeback and again secure the allegiance of men of good will.

With few exceptions, American legal scholars wrongly support the coercive power assumed by the courts in the aftermath of 911 as well as the renewed **"New Deal" delegation** of legislative power to bureaucratically appointed Czars.

The Benthamite misinterpretation of government power as a force for good has destroyed accountable law. Even when we *do* know what the law is, the law becomes subservient to the expansion of personal liability and guilt.

Once under way, it is hard to know where the assault on private property, in the name of public safety and other causes, will stop. What we have done and are doing is to declare open season on property and people through a total separation of liability from fault. We have more in common with the anarchy of the Dark Ages when marauding bands could confiscate whatever they could get their hands on.

Constitutional law has been trivialized. Protection-granting decrees have no basis other than the preference of the judge.

The Constitution has been lost in poor teaching and the legal profession's accommodation to unaccountable power. Never before in history have a people lived in such a hollowed-out legal order as America is today. The American Republic established by the Founding Fathers is long gone, if it ever really was.

The Second Republic under which we now live is a republic in name only. It is governance by bureaucrats who make law under broadly delegated power, and judges who legislate and tax from the bench.

Tyranny is the consequence of unrestrained power, a point that the Founding Fathers well understood when they separated the powers of a small and restrained government. The constitutional issue of our time is the emerging tyranny of unaccountable law.

Breaking News
November 2010

The World Battles The Invasion Of The Naked Body Scanners

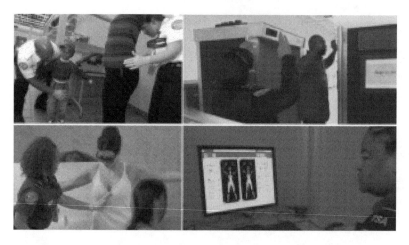

Scientists, pilots, flight attendants, privacy groups, parents, Muslim groups, and everyday passengers, are all rebelling against airport tyranny.

Below are some images taken from the more sophisticated backscatter devices. As you can see, they show all parts of the body in crisp detail.

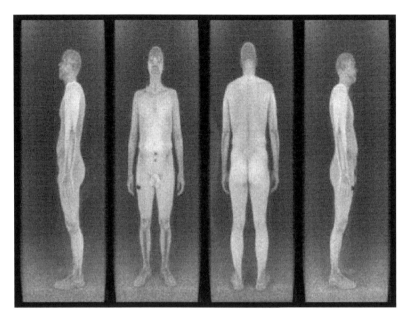

People from all walks of life are rejecting the mass implementation of radiation spewing airport body imaging machines and fighting back against the molestation and groping that women and children are being subjected to at the hands of Transportation Security Administration (TSA) officials.

Multiple pilots' unions are advising their members to avoid the scanners, while simultaneously denouncing the enhanced pat downs as humiliating and on a par with sexual harassment.

The pilots have been joined by flight attendants, with one union demanding that their workers not be touched in sensitive areas in full view of passengers.

Now one of the largest Muslim advice groups, The Council on American-Islamic Relations (CAIR), has issued a warning to all muslims traveling on US aircraft in response to the reports of excessive physical searches of those singled out by security agents and those who refuse to be put through the scanners.

In "special recommendations for Muslim women who wear hijab," CAIR states:

"Before you are patted down, you should remind the TSA officer that they are only supposed to pat down the area in question — in this scenario — your head and neck. They SHOULD NOT subject you to a full-body or partial-body pat-down."

The group also advises that passengers should ask for the procedure to be done in a private place.

Recent accounts from passengers detail the fact that the enhanced body searches are being conducted in public as a way of intimidating others from resisting the scanning machines. They also describe TSA officers in some cases literally lifting travelers from the ground from between the legs and forefully squeezing and feeling around breasts with the fingers and palms of both hands.

As reported by Reuters, parents are now demanding that the procedures be changed for children, after witnesses have described their children's genitals being touched by men and women working for the TSA.

"I didn't think it was going to be as horrible as he was describing," one father noted after an agent told him what he was going to do to the child before conducting the full body search.

"At some point the terrorists have won," the father added. The TSA says it is currently "reviewing" the procedure for children. Perhaps it should first review its policy on background checking its own employees, which by all accounts is woefully inadequate.

While the TSA maintains that the body scanning machines are safe, and that the option of the alternative pat-down will eventually be withdrawn, scientists continue to speak out over the health hazards associated with the x-ray technology.

John Sedat, a University of California at San Francisco professor of biochemistry and biophysics and member of the National Academy of Sciences tells CNet that the machines have "mutagenic effects" and will increase the risk of cancer. Sedat previously sent a letter to the White House science Czar John P. Holdren, identifying the specific risk the machines pose to children and the elderly.

The letter stated:

"It appears that real independent safety data do not exist... There has not been sufficient review of the intermediate and long-term effects of radiation exposure associated with airport scanners. There is good reason to believe that these scanners will increase the risk of cancer to children and other vulnerable populations."

As the following CNN report highlights, the Electronic Privacy Information Center (EPIC), a non-profit privacy advocacy group is currently embroiled in a lawsuit with the TSA over the scanners, arguing that their use is illegal in respect to the 4th Amendment and the documented health risks the machines carry.

All of these groups and individuals will get the chance to speak as one on what has become known as "national opt-out day", scheduled to take place on November 24th. This day of national protest will see thousands and thousands of prople refuse to submit to the tyranny taking over our major airports and scheduled to be implemented on our streets, if we do not resist.

OptOutDay.com declares:

It's the day ordinary citizens stand up for their rights, stand up for liberty, and protest the federal government's desire to virtually strip us naked or submit to an "enhanced pat down" that touches people's breasts and genitals. You should never have to explain to your children, ". . . that no stranger can touch or see your private area, unless it's a government employee; then it's OK."

The goal of National Opt Out Day is to send a message to our lawmakers that we demand change. No naked body scanners, no government-approved groping. We have a right to privacy and buying a plane ticket should not mean that we're guilty until proven innocent.

We urge our readers to join forces with these groups and organize peaceful protests at the nearest airport to you that has implemented body scanners and enhanced TSA pat downs.

The issue has garnered such massive attention, largely due to coverage via **The Drudge Report**, that the federal government has been forced to respond, with TSA Administrator John Pistole and Homeland Security Secretary Janet Napolitano set to meet with executives from the travel industry and heads of pilot associations.

The world is watching.

Sanitary Towel Prompts TSA To Grope Sexual Assault Victim

Forget concealed guns, knives, explosives, the real threat comes from the people.

Menstruating women beware. If you intend to travel, your panty-liners are now considered suspicious objects, after all you could be concealing a bomb in there.

The latest insane TSA transgression answers questions that were raised last week when it was revealed that naked body scanners can also detect sanitary napkins.

New York Times reporter Joe Sharkey wrote Monday that he was getting a lot of requests for information from female frequent fliers.

"Do the imagers, for example, detect sanitary napkins?" women wanted to know. "Yes," wrote Sharkey.

"Does that then necessitate a pat-down? The TSA couldn't say. Screeners, the TSA has said, are expected to exercise some discretion," the article continued.

"And what about tampons?" asked the blog **Feminist Peace Network**. "They look kind of like sticks of dynamite. Are they going to ask us to pull them out and show them just to be sure?"

The answer, judging from one woman's written testimony, seems to be, "Yes."

A customer of the popular women's health company, **Gladrags**, relayed her recent experience at the hands of the TSA, via email.

In short, she was asked to walk through a radiation-projecting naked body scanner and complied. The scanner produced a naked image of her, but because her sanitary towel was obscuring her most intimate parts from prying eyes, the TSA agents pulled her aside for a full groin search. Not something to be relished by any person, let alone someone who has previously suffered sexual assault.

Here is the woman's email testimony in full:

> This email isn't going to be as polished as I would normally send, but I'm upset and I don't want what happened to me to happen to anyone else (if I can stop it).
>
> I recently traveled via air, and was subjected to that new scanning device. "No problem," I thought. I was wearing jeans and a linen tanktop, bra, panties, and one camouflage pantyliner.
>
> I'm a rule follower, so I never have any problems at

the airport. Not this time. I was stopped, and then held for 15 minutes while they tried to find a female supervisor. I couldn't get to my bag, my shawl, or my shoes; just standing there while the TSA agents kept me in one place.

Now, I don't want this to be about bad TSA agents; they were just doing their job, they were as delicate as they could be, etc., etc. But what ultimately happened is that I was subjected to search so invasive that I was left crying and dealing with memories that I thought had been dealt with, years ago, of prior sexual assaults.

Why?

Because of my flannel panty-liner. These new scans are so horrible that if you are wearing something unusual (like a piece of cloth on your panties) then you will be subjected to a search where a woman repeatedly has to check your "groin" while another woman watches on (two in my case – they were training in a new girl – awesome).

So please, please, tell the ladies not to wear their liners at the airport (I didn't even have an insert in). I'm a strong, confident woman; I'm an Army vet (which is why those camo liners crack me up), I work full-time and go to graduate school full-time, I have a wonderful husband, and I don't take any nonsense from anyone. I don't dramatize, and I don't exaggerate. I'm trying to give you a sense of who I am so you won't think that this is a plea for attention, or a jumping on the bandwagon about the recent TSA proposed boycott.

I just don't want another woman to have to go through the "patting down" because she didn't know that her glad-rag would be a matter of national security.

Chalk up another ritual humiliation at the hands of the TSA, "protecting" us from terrorists by forcing women to remove their underwear napkins, and groping their vaginas in public.

When will this insanity end

Mother Kept In "Glass Cage" For Almost An Hour By TSA For Resisting Over Breast Milk

Following their own TSA guidelines will not get you anywhere because they make the rules up as they go along.

The latest case of TSA tyranny to hit the headlines comes in the form of a young mother who was subjected to enhanced groping and then shut inside a screening box for almost an hour by agents after she refused to allow them to put her breast milk through an x-ray device, a legitimate request that is even written into the TSA's own guidelines.

The ordeal, which took place at Phoenix airport, was captured on security cameras, which Stacey Armato, who is also a lawyer, gained access to, but only after repeated requests and careful editing by the TSA had taken place.

After being told that her breast milk might have to be put

through an x-ray scanner, Ms Armato attempted to show the TSA agents a print out of their own guidelines allowing non x-ray screening for breast milk. This act of serious disobedience resulted in the agent pushing Ms Armato into a glass cage, telling her "to be quiet if you know what's good for you", while calling for "back up".

"Standing 50 ft away are the same manager and supervisor I had dealt with the previous week." Ms Armato writes in her description of events, referring to a previous 30 minute delay at the security gate for the exact same reason.

After being shut in the box for some 20 minutes, in full public view of other passengers, Ms Armato began to cry and remonstrate with TSA agents. She was then approached by a police officer who told her that she had been singled out by TSA agents who recognized her because she had filed a complaint against them regarding the handling of her breast milk the previous week.

Ms Armato writes:

> About 10 minutes into all this, a Phoenix PD comes to calm me down. I explain to him that there is no reason I should be treated this way and I have every right to be upset.
>
> He then says "they" (aka TSA) saw me coming, have it out for me (from my complaint against TSA the week before when they didn't know the breast milk rules then either), and I should travel out of a different gate in future weeks.
>
> He said TSA wants me to play along with their horse and pony show and if I don't then, TSA can have the Phoenix PD arrest me! Well, I wanted to get home to my baby and my flight was 30 minutes from departure

so I "played along." Three Phoenix PD watched in the background…I could tell they all knew this was a waste of their time but I was happy to have them standing by in case TSA continued to act out of line.

Eventually Ms Armato was released from the security box, and subjected to a full groping from another TSA agent.

A TSA manager then approached her and told her that the milk had to go through the x-ray scanner because the containers it was in were "too full" and it was "not a clear liquid". These are both made up rules that are not mentioned anywhere in TSA guidelines, proving that even the TSA manager had no regard for the official laws in this instance.

The guidelines allow "Mothers flying with, and now without, their child be permitted to bring breast milk in quantities greater than three ounces as long as it is declared for inspection at the security checkpoint."

According to TSA rules breast milk is to be treated as a medical liquid, which should not be subjected to x-ray radiation.

Ms Armato writes:

> He read the first form which stated that medical liquids can have alternate screening (no x-ray). He was quick to say "well this isn't a medical liquid!" So I had him read the second form which says breast milk is to be treated like a medical liquid. He then says, "well, not today." I started balling all over again once he said that.

Again this is clear evidence of a TSA supervisor acting like a supreme authority and simply making up the rules as he goes along.

Ms Armato was then forced to pour out the milk into 8 different containers, only half filling each, as per the TSA's new completely made up rule.

Because of all this, she missed her flight home to feed her hungry baby in Los Angeles.

The following videos, which show some of the lengthy screening process, were edited together, by Ms Armato with the help of her family. The full unedited set of videos can be viewed at the foot of this article:

According to Ms Armato, the TSA edited out almost 30 minutes of footage, including a section where a TSA manager demanded and took down her personal information, took pictures of her breast milk and shouted at her for not watching closely as the agents tested it for explosive residue.

Ms Armato has vowed to fight the TSA on the issue:

Southwest put me on the next flight home and, as luck would have it, I was standing in line right behind my Constitutional Law Professor from my law school days. At that point I knew I needed to stand up for my rights and help myself and other mothers against the uninformed, retaliatory, and harassing TSA employees that help to **"keep us safe."**

Here is the full set of videos of the incident:

http://tinyurl.com/2b823ds

1. http://tinyurl.com/3yrnv9l
2. http://tinyurl.com/32ffnst
3. http://tinyurl.com/3xhfvf2
4. http://tinyurl.com/389p24x

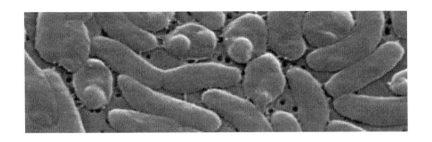

Deadlier Than Scanners: TSA To Spread Disease-Causing Bacteria

Doctors warn of spread of communicable diseases through direct contact with skin; poses far greater risk to public health than statistical chance of being a victim of terrorism.

Now that the TSA's new pat down procedures include reaching inside people's clothing and directly touching their skin and genitals, communicable diseases are set to soar, with doctors warning of a new wave of infections that will pose a greater risk to public health than any statistical probability of being a victim of terrorism.

The TSA's new pat down procedures threaten to unleash an epidemic of communicable diseases, presenting a threat more deadly than the radiation travelers will be exposed to if they pass through a naked body scanner. This will undoubtedly lead to thousands of deaths of people with weak immune systems in the long term.

The controversy again highlights the fact that the body scanner and pat down procedures, through the spread of infectious diseases like flesh-eating bacteria, will kill more people than they will protect through the speculative prevention of any terror attack.

A Different Point Of View

The likelihood of this occurring, now that the TSA have been given free reign to directly grope passengers under their clothing, has greatly increased. The disease can be spread through contact with weakened skin, like a bruise, blister, or abrasion, or merely through minor openings in the skin such as a paper cut or a pin prick.

Cases of flesh-eating bacteria are on the increase and the disease has a 20 per cent death rate.

Syphilis, lice, gonorrhea, ringworm, chlamydia, staph, strep, noro and papilloma viruses are also going to be readily transferred to travelers, since TSA agents do not change gloves between each pat down. Now that screeners are literally touching genitalia, the risk of transmitting sexual diseases will skyrocket.

While people are told to wear flip-flops in the gym or at the swimming pool to prevent infections transmitted via bare feet, the TSA makes people remove their shoes and walk through areas loaded with germs with no protection.

"There is no doubt that bacteria (staph, strep, v.cholerae etc.) and viruses (noro, enteroviruses, herpes, hepatitis A and papilloma viruses) can be spread by contaminated vinyl or latex gloves," Dr. Thomas Warner of Wisconsin told **World Net Daily**.

A pulmonary critical care physician from Connecticut added, "That doesn't make sense that they're not changing gloves."

"Anything can be transmitted if there are open wounds and they [TSA agents] are not aware; there's syphilis, gonorrhea, herpes, chlamydia, lice, ringworm."

"As screening procedures get stricter and more passengers opt for pat-downs instead of graphic X-rays, the likelihood of bacteria being spread increases, Patrick Schlievert, a microbiology and immunology professor at the University of Minnesota Medical School, told **MSNBC**.

Charles Gerba, a microbiology professor at the University of Arizona, found norovirus, MRSA, and influenza virus on the trays that travelers handle before they are subject to pat downs, while self-checkout kiosks were also loaded with germs from thousands of people pushing the same buttons every day.

The TSA and the Centers For Disease Control has failed to respond to growing concerns about TSA gropers spreading infectious diseases.

As we have previously highlighted, the menace of global terrorism has been labeled the greatest threat to western civilization since communism, and yet swimming pools, peanuts and lost deer kill more Americans every single year.

As Ohio State University's John Mueller concludes in a report entitled A False Sense Of Insecurity, "For all the attention it evokes, terrorism actually causes rather little damage and the likelihood that any individual will become a victim in most places is microscopic."

Americans are not only sacrificing their liberty when submitting to invasive and humiliating grope downs at the hands of the TSA, they are in fact putting themselves at a greater health risk statistically of catching a fatal disease than they would ever face from being a victim of terrorism.

TSA Tyranny: ACLU Receives Over 900 Complaints In One Month

Travelers detail purposeful humiliation and violation at hands of federal government.

The American Civil Liberties Union has received a huge wave of complaints within the last month following the TSA security crack down at airports, contradicting the establishment media spin that naked body scanners and invasive pat-downs are being meekly accepted by a compliant public.

"These complaints came from men, women and children who reported feeling humiliated and traumatized by these searches, and, in some cases, comparing their psychological impact to sexual assaults," the **ACLU website** notes.

A Different Point Of View

It states that recurring themes in the hundreds of reports they have received include:
• The searches are extremely invasive;
• Many travelers are reporting intense feelings of violation and humiliation;
• Some report being physically hurt by the searches;
• Some feel their searches are punitive;
• Reports of gawking by agents;
• Reports of seemingly unnecessary repeated touching of intimate areas;
• Many vow not to fly any more;
• Any traveler may be forced to undergo one of these searches.

Following a Freedom of Information request it was recently revealed that to date there were over 600 formal complaints about the use of the naked body scanner devices in airports. Judging from the number of complaints to the ACLU in the last month alone, that number has clearly increased exponentially as the devices, in addition to the new pat-down procedure, have become more widespread.

Comments from passengers subjected to excessive experiences at the hands of the TSA have been published by the ACLU.

"The TSA agent used her hands to feel under and between my breasts," said one woman. "She then rammed her hand up into my crotch until it jammed into my pubic bone."

Another woman described the TSA groping as more invasive than her monthly breast exam with her GP:

"She ran her hands all the way up and into my crotch with force," the woman said. "When she finished with the front she did the same with my back to the point that she, what I would call groped, my butt. She went under, in between, and on my breast."

A New York man described how he was publicly humiliated by TSA agents simply for refusing to go through a scanner:

"Three or four TSA employees came over, basically surrounded me and very loudly proclaimed what a jerk I was for refusing the scan," he said. "The 'supervisor' then spent 15 minutes examining every part of my body – it was intrusive, humiliating and without a shadow of a doubt, intended to punish me for electing to not be irradiated."

The full list of passenger quotations provided by the ACLU can be read at the foot of this article.

Over the past couple of days several corporate media outlets have been running with stories of how the "opt out" protest against the TSA procedures failed to materialize, insinuating that Americans have absolutely no problems with enhanced security measures.

The Boston Herald even suggested that the TSA had been "handed a victory".

However, it soon emerged that the TSA turned off many of its naked body scanners across the country, and scaled back the invasive searches for one day in a hastily crafted PR stunt to mute the impact of the protest.

This move came despite the fact that a TSA administrative directive stated that "Opt-Outters" should be considered "domestic extremists".

In this sense the protest represented a resounding victory for the majority now opposed to TSA tyranny, proving that direct action can influence the government's actions.

The organisers of the protest emphasized this point in a

statement on their website, **optoutday.com**:

Despite claims to the contrary, National Opt-Out Day was a rousing success. The entire point of the campaign was to raise awareness of the issues of privacy and aviation safety at TSA checkpoints, with the ultimate goal of influencing policy – to ask the question "are we really doing this right?" In that, the campaign was a success.

It was always about getting attention to the issue, educating the public and putting pressure on to change the current procedures. With near daily headlines on the front page of newspapers and debates on television and radio news, the mission was accomplished – our voice was heard. By the time November 24 rolled around policy change had already been set in motion.

This success highlights that EVERY day must be an opt-out day, only then will the TSA and the Department of Homeland Security be forced to change the unconstitutional procedures they wish to not only see normalised at airports, but in shopping malls, train stations, and at sports events.

As the **Charlotte Observer** reports, even if airports are pressured to replace the TSA with privately contracted security companies, the TSA procedures will remain. You may not be barked at so loudly, however you will still be faced with a choice of having harmful **ionising radiation** fired at you to produce an image of your naked body, or being felt up by security personnel.

The only way to defeat this tyranny and prevent it spreading to American streets is to follow the example of pilots and flight attendants and flat refuse to submit to it.

More complaints to the ACLU:

(These quotations have been lightly edited for clarity and length. Please be aware that due to the nature of these searches, these complaints often include graphic and sometimes disturbing language.)

I opted out and was sexually molested in public. The method used to search my body was on par with a sexual massage by a stranger of the same sex. My penis was touched by a man. My anus and groin were rubbed by a man. My scalp was rubbed by the same person. How can this be acceptable...? These TSA agents are not qualified to deal with the psychological or ethical responsibility of this technology.

- Joe in New Mexico

The pat down was so invasive that the woman doing it stuck her thumb through my jeans into my vagina, significantly more than simple resistance. She cupped each of my breasts, and ran her hand inside the waistband of my jeans.... I am upset, humiliated, degraded and feel abused and criminal, when I am guilty of nothing.

- Janet from Maryland [no form]

I was visibly upset and when he started to fondle me inappropriately I yelled "I want to see your supervisor!" I asked (emphatically) if he was legally allowed to grab my genitals and the supervisor said he was. After fondling my genitals he groped my buttocks and told me to have a good flight.

- Allen, Nebraska

The TSA agent used her hands to feel under and between my breasts. She then rammed her hand up into my crotch until it jammed into my pubic bone.... I was touched in the pubic region in between my labia.... She then moved her hand across my pubic region and down the inner part of my upper thigh to the floor. She repeated this procedure on the

other side. I was shocked and broke into tears.
- Mary in Texas

In and around breasts, both arms and legs, inside of legs, up to and including genitals (although I clenched the top of my thighs to limit the officer's groping. Legs a second time, but from the rear (where her hand ran up my bum crack). Entire inside waistband of pants, both from the front and rear. Lifted up my hair (already in a ponytail), inside collar of shirt.
- Sharon, Massachusetts

She ran her hands all the way up and into my crotch with force. To get graphic she could have felt if I had a feminine pad on. When she finished with the front she did the same with my back to the point that she, what I would call groped, my butt. She went under, in between, and on my breast. It was more intense than my monthly breast exam.
- Paula M. Hamilton, Corydon, Indiana

In the 4 times she explored the area where my inner thigh met my crotch, she touched my labia each time, and one pass made contact with my clitoris, through 2 layers of clothing. I told her I felt humiliated, assaulted and abused…. In my work as a nurse, if I did what the TSA did against a patient's will it would be considered assault and battery, and I did not see how the TSA should have different rules.
- Chris

TSA says he is going to run the back of his hands on my buttocks and the front of his hands on my groin area…. He feels my bare arms and upper body including my balding scalp. …
- Randy Spencer

This is the most humiliating experience of my entire life. Having another male on his knees in front or behind me and feeling my private areas. And in full view of other passengers. It is a disgusting sight. I now can not sleep due to the thoughts of these agents on their knees feeling my private areas…. I have never, ever been so humiliated and will never, ever fly as long as this policy is in effect.
- Ron Wilson, California

I have a history of having been raped. I was subjected to what I have since learned is a new TSA "enhanced pat down"…. I cried throughout the groping and have had intrusive thoughts since. It was humiliating. I felt powerless. It brought up emotion I could not explain.
- Woman in her 40s

I was shaking and crying the entire time. I was begging them to hurry up but they kept stopping and telling me to calm down. It is impossible to gain composure when a stranger has her hands in your underwear. A crowd gathered and watched and I never felt so humiliated. After it was over, I ran into the ladies' room where I vomited and cried until my plane was boarding.
- Melissa, Massachusetts

I felt molested and sexually harrassed by their search.
- Gweneth from California

I would not hesitate to say that I felt sexually assaulted by the agent.
- Vince from Kansas

This was, by far, the second most humiliating, and personally violating event in my life – the first being a date-rape in college.

— M., Connecticut

The entire affair was very punitive, and humiliating and time consuming and emotionally distressing. When I retrieved my things, I walked into the women's restroom and wept.

— Rosemary, Virginia

While in the "private room"... the agent inappropriately touched my genitalia (more than once) and made me feel incredibly uncomfortable. The agent also pulled down my shorts (about halfway), and I had to ask the agent to let me pull them back up. I was inappropriately touched, groped, rubbed, massaged and sexually harrassed. The procedure was violating, degrading, invasive and humiliating.

— Scott in New Mexico

Simply, I was sexually assaulted. My breasts were caressed in an almost amorous manner. And on the second canvassing of my groin, single-finger pressure was applied to my labia majora — the plane of which was near-broken, during which the agent made a wildly off-color remark.

— B. from Maryland

In all of these years and the thousands of flights and millions of airlines miles I have never been so humiliated. If my choice is to risk having my genitalia spread all over the internet and my body exposed to unknown radiation or to have my testicles bounced and my buttocks stroked I will not fly any commercial airline.... our humanity and our dignity are being violated. I HAVE HAD ENOUGH!

— Dennie from Texas

I am concerned about the exposure and I am equally concerned that someone saw my precious daughter as if she were naked. I was then put through as well and was humiliated and felt as though I were in a peep show. Before this trip, I honestly felt the scanners were a good idea and a price to be paid for travelling – after living it first hand, I have to say it is flat out WRONG.

- Celeste in Florida

The TSA agent did not give me the option of going through the screening machine. She put her hand forcefully in between my legs and took it all the way up into my genital area. She then pressed on my breasts just like a doctor would during a breast exam. She then lifted my dress and put her hands inside of my leggings around my waist…. It was so rough that I felt the effects of it throughout the day.

- Dina Pember, Kennesaw, Georgia

3 or 4 TSA employees came over, basically surrounded me and very loudly proclaimed what a jerk I was for refusing the scan, were laughing at me, repeatedly berating me. The "supervisor" then spent 15 minutes examining every part of my body – it was intrusive, humiliating and without a shadow of a doubt, intended to punish me for electing to not be irradiated.

- Aaron from New York

I was wearing a sanitary napkin, so the agent notified her supervisor that I had a "foreign object." It took about 10 minutes for her to walk 70 feet, speak with the supervisor, and return. Then she collected my carry-ons and began swabbing items in each of them. This process took a verrrrrry long time…. It was obvious to me that this was punitive for refusing the body scanner…. Finally I was told to remove my sanitary napkin. By the time I got to the gate the jetway

A Different Point Of View

had been removed and I was not able to board.
- Suzy in California

Going through the body scanner I said, "I want you to know I do not like this machine. " the TSA agent asked me if I would like to opt out. I said "no, I don't want you to touch me like that, I think it's worse," to which she snickered and replied, "well there's a good chance we're gonna do that anyway." When I went through, she said I did need a pat down, and then she said she need to check my butt and rear crotch.... It was demeaning and indecent....
- Tiffany from Nevada

4 other male and female TSA agents watched while she ran her hands up and down my body, starting with my hair and then going all over, including my breasts and vaginal area.
- A physician, Michigan

My genitals were touched no less than 4 times with the index finger as the screener's hand was slid up my leg until it could go no more into my crotch.
- Marlene, California

This new procedure was absolutely humiliating. She touched my limbs, my torso, my breasts, and rubbed my vagina with her fingers three separate times. I might have understood one rub. Three rubs was NOT acceptable. My pants were thin cotton.... As soon as I left the security area, I began to cry. My husband and I had spent one of the best weeks of our lives together for our honeymoon, and it was destroyed on the way home.
- Tiff, North Carolina

The female TSA agent did not advise me of an alternative and after she directed me through the scanner she conducted the "pat-down" WITHOUT my permission or WITHOUT warning that she would be making direct and forceful contact with my genitals FOUR times! I felt sexually violated and yet afraid to protest for fear that I would be put on some kind of no-fly list or miss my flight.

- Kim, Hawaii

This was a very different and, I maintain, a deliberately abusive experience…. the agent not only felt the inside of my upper thighs but also probed my vagina three separate times. I made it to the end of the search, but then broke down…I cannot and will not allow this to happen to me again…. I continue to have nightmares about this experience.

- Charlotte in California, female, 68

I was with two strangers, one of whom now had both of her open palms moving slowly across virtually every part of my body. She barely moved them as she groped both of my breasts. And most disturbingly, her hands karate-chopped their way a full two inches up into my vagina through my slacks. She performed this maneuver not once, but twice: once from behind me, and then once again, standing/bending in front of me.

- Alex, Washington state

I will do everything in my power to drive rather than take any commercial flights if this is the new standard of TSA screening.

- Max, North Carolina

My daughter was forced to cancel her plans to join us for Thanksgiving because she did not want to subject her children to either the exposure to x-rays or the patdowns. We have cancelled our plans to fly north for Christmas and will drive instead.

- Janet, Florida

The TSA agent squeezes my thighs and runs his hand up until they touched my testicles on both of my legs. This was done in full view of everyone in line. This was very uncomfortable, humiliating and seemed very unnecessary. If given the choice, I will do everything in my power to drive rather than take any commercial flights if this is the new standard of TSA screening.... I do not feel safer. I feel violated....

- Max, North Carolina

When I asked the agent politely for her badge number, she said in a sharp, loud tone, "If you want to know my badge number you can talk to my supervisor!"

- Heather from New York

I have Type 1 Diabetes and wear a wireless insulin pump. TSA supervisors... informed me that since I have to wear a medical device, I will be subject to the enhanced pat-down every time I fly. It's not okay with me to have a stranger grope my genitals once, much less 12-15 times per year. Please, please, please help those of us who are being given no choice in this matter.

- Laura Seay, Georgia

I didn't set off any alarms, apparently I was searched because I was wearing a 'loose fitting shirt'. My T-Shirt was not tucked in.

- Anonymous

I walked through the xray machine… with flying colors. And out of the blue a women said I had to get a pat down.
- Heather from Illinois

I was the only female in a crowd of men. Even though I was not next in line, I was called over to the body scanner. As I got closer to the scanner, I could clearly hear him say "got a cute one, some DD's." … I was appalled and decided at that point to "opt out" of the scanner…. I was then put through the pat down procedure which I only can only describe as sexual assault.
- Caitlin, Connecticut

Americans Trample One Another To Get Their Hands On Cheap Foreign Made Goods

As this past November, 2010, Black Friday clearly demonstrated, Americans are literally willing to trample one another to get the best deals on cheap foreign-made goods. Meanwhile, as thousands of factories and millions of jobs continue to get shipped overseas, the United States is rapidly turning into a post-industrial wasteland.

Once great manufacturing cities such as Camden, New Jersey, have become crime-ridden, gang-infested hellholes.

In some U.S. cities, the "real" unemployment rate is around 30 or 40 percent. The American people desperately need jobs, but the American people are also showing no signs that they plan to give up their addiction to cheap foreign goods.

Our politicians keep insisting that the American people just need "more education" and "more skills" in order to compete, but they don't ever seem to explain how more education and more skills are going to make new jobs pop into existence out of thin air.

The truth is that the American Dream is rapidly becoming the American Nightmare and there is not much hope that any of this is going to turn around any time soon.

The video below is a compilation of video footage from this past Black Friday. It is absolutely shocking to see what average Americans will do to each other just to save a little bit of money on cheap foreign-made goods.

http://tinyurl.com/3xga6uz

Very few of the Americans in the video posted above probably even realize that this wild behavior is destroying our economy a little bit more every day.

Proponents of outsourcing point to all the cheap goods filling our stores as a good thing, but they never tell us about all the good paying American jobs that are being lost.

Sacrificing our industrial base for cheap foreign-made goods is kind of like throwing your furniture into the fire to keep your house warm. We are literally participating in our own economic destruction.

This is a long-term problem that we face. The United States has been running trade deficits for over three decades. Big name corporations are making record profits by shipping our jobs out of the country.

But without good paying jobs, the U.S. middle class simply will not survive.

If anyone can explain how the U.S. middle class is going

to continue to exist without good jobs then please let the rest of us know.

Just look at what is already happening in city after city across the United States.

In a new article entitled "City of Ruins", Chris Hedges does an amazing job of documenting the horrific decline of the city of Camden, New Jersey. Hedges estimates that the real rate of unemployment in Camden is somewhere around 30 to 40 percent, and he makes it sound like nobody in their right mind would want to live there now.

Camden is where those discarded as human refuse are dumped, along with the physical refuse of postindustrial America. A sprawling sewage treatment plant on forty acres of riverfront land processes 58 million gallons of wastewater a day for Camden County. The stench of sewage lingers in the streets. There is a huge trash-burning plant that releases noxious clouds, a prison, a massive cement plant and mountains of scrap metal feeding into a giant shredder. The city is scarred with several thousand decaying abandoned row houses; the skeletal remains of windowless brick factories and gutted gas stations; overgrown vacant lots filled with garbage and old tires; neglected, weed-filled cemeteries; and boarded-up store fronts.

Gangs have stepped into the gaping void left by industry. In Camden today, drugs and prostitution are two of the only viable businesses left – especially for those who cannot find employment anywhere else. The following is how Hedges describes the current state of affairs….

There are perhaps a hundred open-air drug markets, most run by gangs like the Bloods, the Latin Kings, Los Nietos and MS-13. Knots of young men in black leather jackets and baggy sweatshirts sell weed and crack to clients, many of whom drive in from the suburbs. The drug trade is one of the city's few thriving businesses. A weapon, police say, is never more than a few feet away, usually stashed behind a trash can, in the grass or on a porch.

But before we all start judging Camden for being such a horrible place to live, it is important to realize that this is happening in communities from coast to coast. All over the United States industries are leaving and deep social decay is setting in.

If your community is still in good shape right now, be thankful, because what is happening in Camden is going to be happening everywhere soon.

So can anything be done to reverse all this? Well, yes, but right now most of our politicians are standing idly by and are refusing to even speak up about these issues.

Some time ago, CNN ran a series entitled "Exporting America" that looked into the phenomenon of big corporations outsourcing jobs that used to go to Americans.

The United States, once the greatest industrial power on earth, is rapidly becoming a post-industrial nation.

As of the end of 2009, less than 12 million Americans worked in manufacturing. The last time that less than 12 million Americans were employed in manufacturing was in 1941. Meanwhile, our trade deficit continues to soar. Every single month, tens of billions of dollars more goes out of the United States than comes into it. We are literally being drained of our national wealth.

But most Americans could care less about these issues. They just want someone to "fix" things so they are the way they used to be, and they want to be able to continue to get great deals on cheap goods down at the local Wal-Mart.

Unfortunately, the obscene lifestyles that we have all been living are not even close to sustainable. All of this consumerism is going to come crashing down one way or another. Most Americans seem to think that somehow this great bubble of debt can just keep expanding forever, but that is just not possible.

America is in such deep economic trouble that it is hard to even put it into words. Most Americans will not even understand this until the whole thing comes rudely crashing to the ground.

Ultra Elitist Environmental Group Say Halt Economic Growth And Institute Rationing

As fresh UN climate talks begin, de-industrializationists set out their agenda.

Ultra elitist environmental group The Royal Society has published a series of papers to coincide with the latest round of UN climate talks, in which influential scientists suggest that politicians should force the population of the developed world to adhere to a system of rationing in order to stave off the false theory of rising global temperatures.

A Different Point Of View

The papers suggest that 1930s and 40s style crisis rationing should be implemented by Western governments in order to reduce carbon emissions. Such a move would see "limits on electricity so people are forced to turn the heating down, turn off the lights and replace old electrical goods like huge fridges with more efficient models. Food that has travelled from abroad may be limited and goods that require a lot of energy to manufacture," the London Telegraph Reports.

"The Second World War and the concept of rationing is something we need to seriously consider if we are to address the scale of the problem we face," one Royal Society affiliated professor states.

Professor Kevin Anderson, Director of the Tyndall Centre for Climate Change Research, added that in his view, economic growth in the developed world should be completely halted within the next two decades if the planet is to avoid mass upheaval in the form of rising sea levels, floods, droughts and mass migration.

"I am not saying we have to go back to living in caves," he said. "Our emissions were a lot less ten years ago and we got by ok then."

Ironically, Anderson's point here reveals a fundamental flaw in the theory of **anthropogenic warming** (AGW), namely that CO_2 emissions have increased, yet temperature rise is slowing. By all accounts, the warming trend observed predominantly throughout the 1980s and 90s stopped just over a decade ago.

Even the Royal Society itself was forced to admit this fact in a recently published guide, titled 'Climate change: a summary of the science' which was altered following multiple complaints from 43 of the Royal Society's own members that "knowledgeable people" were seeing through brazenly alarmist climate change rhetoric.

The Met office concurs that global warming has been slowing for some time, and the admission was also recently noted by Professor Phil Jones, the figure at the head of the Climategate scandal.

It is hardly surprising to see the Royal Society still pushing a de-industrialization agenda, however, given it's history and cadre of members and patrons.

The Royal Society, a 350 year old establishment outfit, has traditionally been the most vocal proponent for the hypothesis of AGW.

It was the former president of The Royal Society, Lord May, who made the infamous statement "The debate on climate change is over."

When he was head of the Society, May told government advisors: "On one hand, you have the entire scientific community and on the other you have a handful of people, half of them crackpots."

The Royal Society has thrown its full weight behind the global warming movement, lending its absolute support for legislation aimed at reducing carbon emissions by 80%, a process that will devastate the global economy and drastically reduce living standards everywhere.

It has been even more vehement than national governments in its advocacy of the man-made cause of global warming, calling for such drastic CO_2 cuts to be made in the short term, not even by the usual target date of 2050.

Not surprising then that The Royal Society was also intimately tied to efforts to Whitewash the Climategate emails scandal.

A Different Point Of View

The society has also conducted extensive research into geoengineering the planet, and continually lobbies the government to divert funding into it. A recently published lengthy UK Government report drew heavily upon the Society's research and concluded that a global body such as the UN should be appointed to exclusively regulate world wide geoengineering of the planet in order to stave off man made global warming.

This information becomes even more disturbing when you consider the mindset of those who make up the membership of the Society. It is riddled with renowned eco-fascists, open eugenicists and depopulation fanatics.

One notable member is James Lovelock, an eco-fascist who advocates ending democracy and instituting an authoritative elite to oversee global climate management and a radical stemming of the human population in order to combat climate change. He is also a patron of the Optimum Population Trust, a notorious UK-based public policy group that campaigns for a gradual decline in the global human population, which it refers to as "primates" or "animals", to what it sees as a "sustainable" level.

Lovelock is also an ardent advocate of geoengineering. In 2007 Lovelock proposed laying vast swathes of pipes under the world's oceans in order to pump water from the bottom of the seas – rich in nutrients, but mostly dead – to the top. The idea being that the action would encourage algae to breed, absorb more carbon and release more dimethyl sulphide into the atmosphere, a chemical known to seed sunlight reflecting clouds. Such methods are also covered in the Commons report.

Another member is Jonathon Porritt, former chair of the UK Sustainable Development Commission, one of former

Prime Minister Gordon Brown's leading green advisers, who has stated that Britain's population must be cut in half from around 60 million to 30 million if it is to build a sustainable society.

Porritt, also a member of the Optimum Population Trust, a connection that caused raised eyebrows when it was announced that Porritt was to be a part of a forthcoming Royal Society "Objective" Global Population Study.

Also on the Royal Society's working group for their global population study is another of their patrons, and another OPT member, BBC darling wildlife broadcaster and filmmaker Sir David Attenborough. Attenborough has called for a one child policy like that of Communist China to be implemented in Britain. The proposal is one of the OPT's main initiatives. Again, how is this man's influence going to result in an "objective" study on population?

Another member of that working group is Cambridge economist Sir Partha Dasgupta, also a fellow of the OPT.

Professor Malcolm Potts, another member of the working group was the first male doctor at the Marie Stopes Abortion Clinic in London, he also advised on the UK's 1967 Abortion Act.

Marie Stopes was a prominent campaigner for the implementation of eugenics policies. In Radiant Motherhood (1920) she called for the "sterilisation of those totally unfit for parenthood [to] be made an immediate possibility, indeed made compulsory." That group, according to her, included non-whites and the poor.

Stopes, an anti-Semite Nazi sympathizer, campaigned for selective breeding to achieve racial purity, a passion she shared with Adolf Hitler in adoring letters and poems that she sent the leader of the Third Reich.

Stopes also attended the Nazi congress on population science in Berlin in 1935, while calling for the "compulsory sterilization of the diseased, drunkards, or simply those of bad character." Stopes acted on her appalling theories by concentrating her abortion clinics in poor areas so as to reduce the birth rate of the lower classes.

Stopes left most of her estate to the Eugenics Society, an organization that shared her passion for racial purity and still exists today under the new name The Galton Institute. The society has included members such as Charles Galton Darwin (grandson of the evolutionist), Julian Huxley and Margaret Sanger.

Perhaps most notably, the head of the Royal Society's new study, John Sulston, most famously played a leading role in the **Human Genome Project**, the effort to identify and map the thousands of genes of the human genome. Sulston worked under James D. Watson, a notorious eugenicist who has previously argued that black people are inherently less intelligent than whites and has advocated the creation of a "super-race" of humans, where the attractive and physically strong are genetically manufactured under laboratory conditions. Watson is also affiliated with the Royal Society, indeed, in 1993 he received the society's Copley Medal of honour for "outstanding achievements in research in any branch of science, and alternates between the physical sciences and the biological sciences".

Sulston is also a leading advocate of the renowned Atheist group, The British Humanist Association.

It is clear that this organisation and these people are immersed in the science of eugenics, and that they have continued the science under the guise of environmentalism. They hate humanity and any notion that their studies will represent anything other than an establishment avocation of mass depopulation is farcical.

Given the standing of the Royal Society and its ability to influence policy making on an international scale, it is imperative that the media, places of education, government representatives and the wider public are made aware of these facts

IPCC Professor Calls For "Elite Warrior Leadership" To Rule Over Ecological Dictatorship

Prominent United Nations scientists says new green religion should replace traditional faiths as part of shift towards authoritarian tyranny.

An influential professor who worked as an assessor for the United Nations **Intergovernmental Panel on Climate Change** (IPCC) has called for **democracy** to be replaced with an **eco-dictatorship** where enslaved masses are ruled over by an "elite warrior leadership" and forced to adhere to a new "green religion," in yet another shocking example of how prominent global warming alarmists are revealing themselves as dangerous eco-fascists.

A Different Point Of View

Professor David Shearman, MD, is Emeritus Professor of Medicine, University of Adelaide, and a Visiting Research Fellow at the University's Department of Geography and Environmental Sciences and Law School. Shearman was an Assessor for the IPCC's Third Assessment and Fourth Assessment Reports.

In his writings, Shearman, who labels humanity a "malignant eco-tumour" and an "ecological cancer," says that "authoritarianism is the natural state of humanity" and that in order to save the planet from man-made climate change, an "elite warrior leadership" needs to be formed that will "battle for the future of the earth".

Part of this battle involves replacing traditional religions like Christianity and Islam with a new "green religion" that would fit better with an authoritarian government.

"It is not impossible, from the green movement and aspects of the new age movement, that a religious alternative to Christianity and Islam emerge," writes Spearman, in The Climate Change Challenge and the Failure of Democracy. "And it is not too difficult to imagine what shape this new religion could take. Such would require a transcendent God who could punish and reward — because humans seem to need a carrot and a stick."

Spearman's "transcendent God" is the God of the State, punishing the enslaved citizen for every eco-infraction under this new green totalitarianism. Spearman openly advocates the contrived manufacturing of a new God and a new religion so that the masses of enslaved citizens under his envisaged "eco-autocracy" would be coerced to comply as part of some hideous global brainwashing program. This obviously has its roots in ancient pagan beliefs of barbaric sacrifices being necessary to appease Mother Earth, which at one stage in history involved mothers killing their own babies for the greater good.

Even more chillingly, Shearman advocates the setting up of specialized "re-education centers" where eco-zombies would be trained to become part of a "green army" of enforcers.

"Chapter 9 will describe in more detail how we might begin the process of constructing such universities to train the eco-warriors to do battle against the enemies of life. We must accomplish this education with the same dedication used to train its warriors. As in Sparta, these natural elites will be especially trained from childhood to meet the challenging problems of our times," writes Spearman.

Spearman outlines his vision of a dictatorial global government comprised of the elite ruling over the planet, on page 134.

"Government in the future will be based upon . . . a Supreme office of the Biosphere. The office will comprise specially trained philosopher/ecologists. These Guardians will either rule [by] themselves or advise an authoritarian government of policies based on their ecological training and philosophical sensitivities. These Guardians will be specially trained for the task."

"Posted on a blog somewhere, such a plan would probably elicit a visit from the anti-terrorist division of the police," writes *Haunting The Library blog.* "But the fact that it comes from a professor at a major university, who works for the IPCC and was written at the behest of a serious academic institute, founded by [an] Act of Congress, means that the author need not be afraid. But we should be."

"I could go on quoting from the book, but I'm sure you've already got the gist of what's being proposed here: Global warming presents such a massive and immediate danger that democracy no longer cuts it, and an authoritarian ecological government of **'natural elites'** will have to be found to replace it, as well as a new green religion to help provide 'social glue for the masses'."

As we have documented, Shearman is not alone in his brazen call for freedom to be abolished and replaced by an authoritarian green tyranny. Indeed, this is a common cause embraced by a multitude of influential climate change activists and scientists.

• Finnish environmentalist guru and global warming alarmist Pentti Linkola has publicly called for climate change deniers to be "re-educated" in eco-gulags, and that the vast majority of humans be killed, with the rest enslaved and controlled by a green police state, with people forcibly sterilized, cars confiscated, and travel restricted to members of the elite. Linkola wants the last 100 years of human progress to be "destroyed".

• James Lovelock, the creator of the Gaia hypothesis, told the *Guardian* last year that "democracy must be put on hold" to combat global warming and that "a few people with authority" should be allowed to run the planet.

• This sentiment was echoed by author and environmentalist Keith Farnish, who in a recent book called for acts of sabotage and environmental terrorism in blowing up dams and demolishing cities in order to return the planet to the agrarian age. Prominent NASA global warming alarmist and Al Gore ally, Dr. James Hansen, endorsed Farnish's book.

• The current White House science czar John P. Holdren also advocates the most obscenely dictatorial, eco-fascist, and inhumane practices in the name of environmentalism. In his 1977 Ecoscience textbook, Holdren calls for a "planetary regime" to carry out forced abortions and mandatory sterilization procedures, as well as drugging the water supply, in an effort to cull the human surplus.

• Another prominent figure in the climate change debate who exemplifies the violent and death-obsessed belief system of the movement is Dr. Eric R. Pianka, an American biologist based at the University of Texas in Austin. During a speech to the Texas Academy of Science in March 2006, Pianka advocated the need to exterminate 90% of the world's population through the airborne ebola virus.

If you want to get a taste of what it would be like to live under Shearman's eco-dictatorship, just take a look at the following video, **Planned-opolis**, which promotes the imposition of literal **hi-tech prison cities** where populations have their food and travel rationed by an all-powerful State that regulates every aspect their existence and incarcerates refusniks inside **squalid ghettos**.

Planned-opolis
http://tinyurl.com/236t3so

Eco-Fascists Call For Prison Cities

Obey enviro-tyranny or be banished to the ghetto; new government-funded propaganda piece threatens.

People who resist the State controlling every aspect of their existence will be forced to live in squalid ghettos while the rest of the population will be tightly controlled in high-tech prison cities – that's the future envisaged by eco-fascists who are exploiting the contrived global warming fraud to openly flaunt their plan for the total enslavement of mankind.

The threat posed by the kind of scenario being promoted by *Forum for the Future,* the group responsible for the chilling video below, cannot be emphasized enough. The dictatorial hellhole of 2040, where cars will be banned, meat rationed, farming completely abolished and overtaken by the state, behavior catalogued on "calorie cards," and careers

A Different Point Of View   177

ordained by the government, is the ultimate goal of the control freaks who have seized the reigns of the environmental movement.

Nearly every aspect of the policies undertaken by the global dictatorship that runs the **"planned-opolis"** depicted in the video are lifted wholesale from historical tyrannies.

• The state completely taking over the means of food production and farming. This is a throwback to the Soviet system of collectivized farming, where Stalin organized land and labor into large-scale collective farms. Farmers who resisted the state taking over their farms were arrested and sent to Siberian gulags. As a result of the mass seizure of property and the disruption that collective farming brought to food production, upwards of 3 million people died from starvation from 1932-33 alone. A similar system imposed in Maoist China under the "Great Leap Forward" led to the Great Chinese Famine and the starvation of at least 36 million people.

• The incarceration of Resistors to green fascism inside squalid ghettos and their subsequent separation from family members is a frightening throwback to the Nazi-run Warsaw Ghetto and other concentration camps and prisons within cities that housed Jews and political dissidents during World War Two.

• The restriction or even outlawing of meat, something already being vehemently pushed by eco-fascists, to the point where a hamburger becomes a rare delicacy to be enjoyed on special occasions — and only then if you can afford it. As my friend's wife who is Chinese will attest, up until the late 802s before China started to lift itself out of poverty, meat was a rare treat that was sparsely available and highly restricted. Again, the **"planned-opolis"** is nothing less than a fusion of Communist and fascist control measures inflicted upon the population to keep them poor, starving and weak.

The people who produced this video, funded by monolithic elitist banks and corporations like Royal Dutch Shell and Bank of America, as well as the British government, know very well that every aspect of their **"planned-opolis"** is lifted directly from the most abhorrent and brutal dictatorships in history. They are openly flaunting the neo-fascist ideology behind the green movement.

Of course, as is made clear in the video, none of these regulations or controls will apply to any of the elitists imposing them on the rest of us. Think, Al Gore and his multiple oceanside mansions with heated swimming pools. They will still be able to roll around in SUV's and fly private jets while quaffing the finest fillet steak and belching tons of CO_2 as they lecture the rest of humanity about their carbon footprint. Think, Prince Charles and his insistence that the "proles" not be allowed to take baths, as he lounges in the luxuriant splendor of royal palaces.

They are also engaged in a ploy to shift the parameters of the Overton Window - which is defined as "A range of policies considered to be politically acceptable in the current climate of public opinion." By constantly bombarding us with extreme and repugnant proposals, they gradually wear down the human psyche until people begin to accept draconian controls over their personal life as normal, necessary and reasonable.

This is part of the reason behind last year's **"splattergate"** controversy, where global warming alarmists – again funded by government and big business – produced an infomercial in which children who refused to lower their carbon emissions were slaughtered in an orgy of blood and guts.

This is a psychological attack and a realization of the stepping stone method to tyranny. Whereas we might not accept cars being banned and meat being rationed now, we will accept incandescent light bulbs being outlawed and paying carbon taxes on fuel. As each hurdle is cleared, the globalists propose something more extreme so that we will always come to a compromise and accept a slighter lesser tyranny, but in the long term, the elitists achieve all of their goals with aplomb.

And to top it all off, the debate between the "liberals" over at the *Guardian* website in response to this story did not revolve around a castigation of this authoritarian future hell, but a question of whether old people should merely be advised by government workers how to kill themselves when they reach 65, or whether the state should just kill them directly.

This kind of despotic destiny is not only being pushed by the elite, it has an army of greenwashed zombies behind it who have been recruited to make the **democide of the elderly** (the useless eaters) an intellectually acceptable and reasonable idea. Presumably, the disabled and the mentally ill will also be exterminated in the pursuit of a highly efficient **"planned-opolis,"** another idea of which Hitler would have vehemently approved.

Once government is given the power to kill anyone they deem to be unproductive in this **collectivist Orwellian nightmare,** the gates of hell are thrown wide open. In comparison, meat rationing, carbon taxes, eco-surveillance, calorie credits and transport restriction will seem like a walk in the park.

Alex Jones' seminal film **Endgame,** released in 2007, warned precisely of the kind of **hi-tech slave grids** being implemented that are now routinely proposed by top eco-fascist organizations. We urge you to warn everyone you know about this agenda and to stand up in unison to resist the first great assault on human liberty of the 21st century, which is now certain to be inflicted on us under the guise of saving mother earth. We either stop this now, or we end up in the eco-ghettos that our masters have readied for us in their **"planned-opolis"** of 2040.

Communi-city
http://tinyurl.com/27bt5y8

Planned-Opolis: Elitist Agenda For Eco-Enslavement

Chilling future scenario funded by banks & oil companies depicts **authoritarian cities** where only the wealthy will be allowed to eat meat, drive cars, and choose their own career – all in the name of preventing non-existent global warming.

Not content with depicting children being slaughtered in the name of preventing non-existent global warming . . .
http://tinyurl.com/2ea62k9
. . . climate change alarmists have embarked on a new propaganda campaign lecturing us all about how we will be forced to live in a **"planned-opolis,"** where car use will be heavily restricted, CO2 emissions will be rationed, meat will be considered a rare delicacy, the state will decide your career, and only the **mega-rich elitists** enforcing all these new rules and regulations will be exempt from them.

Browbeating us about how the only solution to expensive fossil fuels is to enforce a "tightly planned and controlled" system, the infomercial (funded in part by oil companies like Royal Dutch Shell), goes on to tell the story of what life will be like in 2040 through the words and actions of a subservient, obedient slave named "Vee" who dutifully acquiesces to the necessity of the new way of things.

Even as Britain shivers under its coldest December in 100 years, and as places as far flung as Southern China suffer unprecedented bouts of freezing rain and cold weather and as the onset of a new mini ice age causes mass die-offs of sea life, the entire piece, produced by the *Forum for the Future* group, is veiled in debunked rhetoric about CO_2 emissions causing rising temperatures.

We soon begin to learn what living in the new **"planned-opolis"** will look like – food and water is regulated and rationed by a **"Global Food Council"** which seizes total control over farming. Meat is a rare treat only to be enjoyed on special occasions (mirroring precisely the conditions endured by those in Maoist China).

The state decides what your job will be with "designated career announcements," nobody has the choice to decide their own vocation.

Movement and behavior is controlled by a **calorie credit card** linked to a smart phone that rations the amount of travel the citizens of **slave-opolis**, I mean **"planned-opolis,"** are allowed to make. Private ownership of cars will be banned for non-elitists because, "the state knows they just aren't practical anymore."

Of course, none of these new rules will apply to the rich elitists enforcing them on the rest of us – it's made clear in the ad that the wealthy will still be able to roll around in CO_2-belching cars whenever they like while everyone else is forced to get government permission and be allocated a time slot in which to use restricted vehicles provided by the "Slick Travel Corporation".

"It makes so much sense doesn't it," insists the smiley faced slave "Vee," who enjoys the fact that she can "switch off brain and go to work," adding, "With this many people around I'm glad there's a mega-computer in charge."

Of course, for those who resist and still cling to some semblance of freedom in defiance of the state and the super-computers running the slave grid, there's the **"cry freedom ghetto,"** prison camps for malcontents who are blocked from getting jobs, accessing high speed transport, or the Internet.

In a chilling throwback to the concentration camps of Nazi Germany, the **propaganda piece** chillingly invokes the notion of families being separated because some people refuse to submit to state-imposed green fascism. This is a subtle yet shocking insight into the true motivation of the makers of this piece – they can barely contain their wanton revulsion towards freedom and their fascist tendencies.

The *Forum for the Future Organization* derives its funding from a combination of taxpayer money, via local governments, as well as monolithic corporations and large banks.

Some of its financial backers include Bank of America, the City of London Corporation, PepsiCo UK, Time Warner, and crucially Royal Dutch Shell – which of course is one of the biggest emitters of CO_2 on the planet.

In other words, an organization lecturing the little people about how only the mega-rich will be able to drive cars and eat meat in 30 years in order to reduce CO_2 emissions is largely funded by mega-rich banks and multinational corporations, as well as oil companies.

This is nothing less than *Orwell's 1984* and then some – a chilling nightmare scenario where all freedom is crushed in the name of protecting mother earth. But of course, this

A Different Point Of View

has nothing to do with saving the environment, the whole thing is funded by multinational corporations and giant banks, and yet the idiot "liberals" over at the Guardian website wholeheartedly agree that rationing, government control of mobility and food, the state deciding your career, cars being banned for all but the rich, and resistors forced to live in abandoned ghettos is a reasonable and rational course of action.

The agenda for eco-fascism knows no bounds – despite the fact that global warming has been completely discredited as a contrived fraud based on pseudo-science, corruption and agenda-driven politics, its adherents are relentlessly forging ahead with their horrifying vision of a future where the middle classes are eviscerated and everyone – besides of course the elitists imposing the tyranny – is forced to reduce their living standard and become subservient to an all-pervading state that enforces high-tech slavery under the excuse of a green revolution.

Banning incandescent light bulbs and introducing carbon taxes is only the beginning – if we let these parasites have their way with us we'll all be living in their purpose built slave-opolis before we know it.

Renew-abad
http://tinyurl.com/23r4nr9

Eco-Nazi Orders Americans To Pay Carbon Tax On Children

IPCC Professor wants communist-style controls on giving birth.

Top United Nations Eco-Nazi Professor David Shearman isn't content with forcing the planet to worship a new green God while accepting the abolition of freedom and its replacement with an authoritarian global government run by "elite warriors," he also wants Americans to pay a carbon tax of more than $18,000 dollars for each CO_2 exhaling, Mother Earth killing child they have.

In an article first published in January, 2011, we learned how Shearman, Emeritus Professor of Medicine at the University of Adelaide and Assessor for the Intergovernmental Panel on Climate Change (IPCC) Third and Fourth Assessment Reports, wants to dispense with democracy and replace it with an **"authoritarian government"** run by elite "eco-guardian warriors" who will invent a new green religion to coerce the "proles" into following their every order in the name of saving the planet.

A Different Point Of View

We are now starting to get a clearer picture of how the "elite warriors" in control of this enviro-dictatorship will dominate every aspect of human society, down to the very act of procreation itself.

In an article posted on the *Doctors for the Environment Australia (DEA)* website (of which he is President), Shearman laments the fact that "behavior modification" by global warming alarmists is not working because most people have been brought up in "liberal democracies" that allow them some semblance of freedom. He calls for, "Enforced rules whether at the collective level through carbon trade with penalties OR at the individual level."

"The first step to overcoming this obstacle, Professor Shearman writes, is persuading the governments of the world that curtailing the right to have children is an absolutely essential part of the fight against global warming," points out *HauntingTheLibrary* blog.

Shearman quotes a letter that appeared in the *Medical Journal of Australia* which discusses how **children having the temerity to breathe** is harming the planet and that "population control" needs to be enforced as part of a "second ecological revolution".

In a subsequent article entitled, *Please Pay the Climate Change Tax on Your Children*, Shearman argues that this new green revolution should be funded by a carbon tax on those who dare to break Communist-style one child policies enforced by his yearned for totalitarian global government. Under the notorious one child policy in China, women who defy its edicts are sent to **"re-education camps,"** once they have been beaten, forcibly injected and had their baby boiled alive inside their womb, of course.

"Every family choosing to have more than a defined number of children should be charged a carbon tax that would fund the planting of enough trees to offset the carbon cost generated by a new human being," he writes. "They should pay 5,000 dollars (4,400 US) a head for each extra child and up to 800 dollars every year thereafter."

"Over 18 years, that works out to a climate change child tax of approximately $18,800 US. Professor Shearwater doesn't comment on what penalties would be imposed on couples failing to pay the tax. Perhaps confiscation is a possibility. Who knows?" asks *HauntingTheLibrary*.

The agenda for a global one child policy is being advanced by billionaire elitists who are exploiting the contrived climate change scam to push for total control over mankind.

In a May 2009 confab in London, a gaggle of rich "philanthropists," including David Rockefeller, Ted Turner, Bill Gates, Warren Buffet and George Soros met to discuss ways of "solving overpopulation".

As we have tirelessly documented, "population control" has nothing to do with saving the planet – the United Nations' own figures show that world population will level out at 9 billion and then make a rapid decline.

In reality, what is now termed population control is merely a disguise for the barbaric and arcane race-based theories of eugenics, which were exported out of Britain where they originated by Rockefeller's father, John D. Rockefeller, to Nazi Germany, where they were cited by Hitler as a justification for the holocaust, the sterilization of so-called defectives and state-sanctioned mass murder of disabled people.

Sprawl-ville
http://tinyurl.com/27fck6y

Somewhere in America, a seventeen-year-old boy is living the last year of his life.

As America Nears All-Out Civil War

A new Russian Foreign Intelligence Service (SVR) report circulating in the Kremlin warns today that the long-feared-for new American Civil War may be now underway after shots fired from what are believed to be high-powered military-type sniper rifles shattered windows in the Pentagon and in the nearby Marine Corps National Museum, both located in the Washington D.C. area of the United States.

According to this report, more than 6 shots were fired by an unidentified sniper team targeting the Pentagon and shattering a number of windows, following 3 days of a similar attack on the Marine Corps National Museum where 5 shots destroyed the double-pained-glass windows in that building's atrium.

Astoundingly, US security officials described these attacks as "a random event," but which the director of the civilian Pentagon Force Protection Agency (PFPA), Steven Calvery, said would have to be "re-evaluated" if in their investigation they find the incident to be part of a larger plot.

The SVR report, however, points out these attacks on the most protected city in the world bear all the hallmarks of sophisticated and highly trained sniper-teams probing the defenses of its more powerful foe and employing the tactics of "relocation" and "sound masking."

"Relocation" involves firing a few shots from a certain position, with snipers moving unseen to another location before the enemy can determine where he is and mount a counterattack, and "Sound Masking" is the technique of using loud sounds in the environment (in both of these cases passenger jet takeoffs from Ronald Reagan Washington National Airport) that can mask the sound of the shot. Both of these techniques are frequently used in clandestine operations, infiltration tactics, and guerrilla warfare.

Raising the fears of the Americans, this report continues, are events occurring in France where that Nations population has begun to target their elite classes, and, as we can read, in part, as reported from Paris:

"Youths who pillaged stores, torched cars and fought street battles with police, have transformed the genteel French city of Lyon into a flashpoint of violence over an unpopular pension reform.

"One of France's wealthiest cities, and more commonly associated with fine-dining than riots, Lyon has seen the worst violence of these protests as clashes injured two dozen people and scores more were arrested."

In explaining the growing fears of America's elite over

the rising anger in their country, New York Times writer Robert H. Franks, in his editorial titled *Income Equality: Too Big to Ignore,* warned:

"In a recent working paper based on census data for the 100 most populous counties in the United States, researches in political science and economics found that the counties where income inequality grew the fastest also showed the biggest increases in symptoms of financial distress.

For example, even after controlling other factors, these counties had the largest increases in Bankruptcy filings."

Even worse, perhaps, was Time Magazine's warning in an article titled "Will the Federal Reserve Cause a Civil War?"...that American stands on the cusp of total rebellion and as we can, in part, read:

"What is the most likely cause today of civil unrest? Immigration? Gay Marriage? Abortion? The results of the next election? The Mosque at Ground Zero? No... Try the Federal Reserve. November 3rd is when the Federal Reserve's next policy committee meeting ends, and if you thought this was just another boring money meeting you would be wrong. It could be the most important meeting in Fed history.

"As we had previously outlined in our October 7th report, 'Obama Set To Flee America As Us Dollar Faces 50% Devaluation,' global economic stability is so near to crashing that the World Bank issued and unprecedented warning that, in part, said:

"Surging capital inflows threaten Asia's economic stability, the World Bank warned; a day after Treasury Secretary Timothy Geithner sought to draw the venom from a global row over currencies by vowing not to devalue the dollar.

"US Treasury Secretary Timothy Geithner then, perplexingly, told the American media that 'a weaker dollar

A Different Point Of View

may now be in the national interest.'"

China's actions against the United States were predictable, immediate and harsh with that country's Communist government ordering an immediate halt to the sale of vital rare earth metals to the Americans in a blow to the US industries dependant upon them to keep running.

China also ordered its Naval patrol boats back to the Japanese administered islands (known as Senkaku in Japan, and Diaoyu in China) that they had just left, and threatening a conflict with the United States who has vowed to protect the islands under its treaties with the Japanese.

This SVR report stated that China's actions are based upon their belief that the Americans will soon no longer be able to project their power overseas as it becomes bogged down by the masses of its people who have not only lost all confidence in their government, but believe that all of their elite associated with Washington are, in fact, destroying their country.

And if the American people needed any further proof of the disdain they are held in by their Washington and moneyed elite, it came in a shocking report stating that the very banks that these people had just bailed out to the tune of more than $1 Trillion dollars have now turned utterly and completely against them.

As we can read, in part, as reported by the Huffington Post:

"Nearly a dozen major banks had hedge funds anticipating quick profits from homeowners who fall behind on property taxes are quietly plowing hundreds of millions of dollars into businesses that collect the debts, tack on escalating fees, and threaten to foreclose on the homes of those who fail to pay.

The Wall Street investors, which include Bank of America and J.P. Morgan Chase & Co., have purchased from local governments the right to collect delinquent taxes on several hundred thousand properties, many in distressed housing markets, the Huffington Post Investigative Fund has found.

In may cases, the banks and hedge funds created new companies to do their bidding. They gave the companies obscure, even whimsical names and used post office boxes as their addresses to mask Wall Street's dominant new role as a surrogate tax collector.

In exchange for paying overdue real estate taxes to local governments, the investors gain legal powers from the local governments to collect the debts and levy collection and other fees.

At first property owners may owe little more than a few hundred dollars, only to find their bills souring into the thousands. In some jurisdictions, the new Wall Street tax collectors also chase debtors over other small bills, such as for water, sewer, and sidewalk repair.

To the reaction of those American people who *do* realize what is happening to them we can further read, as reported by PrisonPlaner.Com News Service:

"Americans are acquiring guns, silver, and going on food stamps, at record levels in reaction to the crumbling economy; trends indicative of a fearful public who are struggling financially and preparing for potential mass civil unrest in the aftermath of a total economic collapse.

"FBI records and Google Trends research show that firearms purchases are still at record highs, but that ammunition sales have leveled off, suggesting that a flood of first-time gun owners have rushed to protect themselves from the potential of higher crime and even civil unrest in the event of a widespread financial meltdown.

"That tells us that there are more first-time gun buyers coming in to buy firearms, and that speaks to our worries about security. They buy a few rounds of ammunition first time, but they don't buy more; ConvergEx Group Chief Market Strategist Nicholas Colas told CNBC."

In their recent article titled "The Secret World of Extreme Militias," Time Magazine further warns that hundreds of thousands, if not millions, of Americans are now actively training to confront any police or military forces thrown against them by their Washington backed elite; a grim circumstance further substantiated by the Federal Bureau of Investigation (FBI) reporting that over 57,000 US police officers were attacked in 2009 showing the full extent of the breakdown of law and order in a nation undergoing total economic collapse.

Important to note in this Russian SVR report, too, is the "most likely" scenario of how the battle for the very soul of the United States will unfold, and which eerily nearly matches the one prepared by one of Russia's top diplomats who has long warned that 2010 may very well be the year America splits apart for good, and as we can, in part, read as reported by the Wall Street Journal News Service:

"For a decade, Russian academic Igor Panarin has been predicting that the U.S. will fall apart in 2010. For most of that time, he admits, few took his argument, that an economic and moral collapse will trigger a civil war and the eventual breakup of the U.S., very seriously. Now he's found an eager audience: Russian state media.

"In recent weeks, he's been interviewed as much as twice a day about his predictions. 'It's a record,' says Prof. Panarin. 'But I think the attention is going to grow even stronger.'"

"Prof. Panarin, 50 years old, is not a fringe figure. A former KGB analyst, he is dean of the Russian Foreign Ministry's academy for future diplomats.

"Panarin is invited to Kremlin receptions, lecture students, publishes books, and appears in the media as an expert on U.S.-Russian relations."

The great American Revolutionary War Hero and the United States' supposed first President, George Washington, once warned his people, "Government is not reason; it is not eloquent; it is force. Like fire, it is a dangerous servant and a fearful master."

The lessons for Washington and America's moneyed elite, though, will be much worse because, according to the SVR Russian report; if the United States was unable to win the Vietnam War against an essentially peasant army on a land mass of 128,527 square miles with nearly 1 million troops, how could it even *begin* to confront an armed uprising in just one of its States like Montana that has a land mass of 147,165 square miles and an armed population of nearly 1 million anti-government citizens?

To all of these dire events now occurring in the United States, which are already shaking the entire world, the best guidance for protection is knowledge, and perhaps, are most succinctly found in the book, "The Fourth Turning," whose authors note:

"The future is only the past again; entered through another gate."

Increasingly Americans are sensing that the next great gate in history is approaching. It's time to trust our instincts, think seasonally, and prepare.

"Forewarned is forearmed."

People Yearning to be Free Courageously Resist Tyranny

Nothing touches the heart more profoundly than when a people yearning to be free courageously resist tyranny.

Since the turn of the 17th Century, there have been thousands of memorable instances of extraordinary courage and determination by people willing to pay the ultimate price for freedom.

Some of those instances come with symbolism so profound that they stand out as historic markers of man's unending quest to get freed of the shackles from government.

Here are a few of those instances, ones that affected all of humanity at the time they occurred and continue to linger in human consciousness, beckoning us to be vigilant in defense of those same liberties today:

1. The toppling of the statue of King George III in Bowling Green, New York City;

2. The lone unarmed protestor in Tiananmen Square facing down a column of tanks;

3. President Ronald Reagan at the Brandenburg Gate beseeching Mikhail Gorbechev to "Tear down this wall."

The Toppling of the Statue of King George III

On August 21, 1770, in Bowling Green, New York City (at what is now Broadway in lower Manhattan), agents of the Crown erected a 4,000 pound gilded lead statue of King George III wrapped in the Roman garb of an emperor riding atop a powerful stallion.

The statue invited spectators to be humbled by the monarch's absolute power.

The colonists refused the invitation.

Joseph Wilton from London designed the statue at the Crown's request to fill the colonists with a sense of awe and deference for the Hanoverian King; instead, the statue became a focal point for colonial protests against British oppression.

Offended by the impositions of laws that would tax and regulate them without their representation in Parliament and require tax payment in gold and silver, colonists desecrated the base of the statue with graffiti expressing their revulsion of the monarchical tyranny.

In 1773, the colonial government of New York enacted an anti-graffiti law and encircled the statue with a protective cast-iron fence.

Atop each fence post were miniature cast iron crowns, that angry colonists cut off several of the posts.

On July 9, 1776, upon hearing the Declaration of Independence read for the first time on the steps of City Hall in New York, certain of General George Washington's troops, Sons of Liberty, and interested by-standers transformed their elation into a riot, racing down Broadway to Bowling Green, aiming to vent their rage against imperial tyranny.

The head of George III was severed from the body of the statue. Certain of the protestors then paraded it about New York on a pike staff, and sawed the remainder of the statue into pieces.

At the direction of Declaration signer Oliver Walcott, Sr., certain portions were then shipped to a Connecticut foundry and melted to form 42,088 patriot bullets.

Once part of the statue heralding the reign of an absolute monarch, the bullets were donated to Federal Washington's army as ammunition to shoot at British regulars.

No doubt some British soldiers died with lead in their bodies supplied from the statue of British King George III.

The Lone Unarmed Protestor in Tiananmen Square Facing Down a Column of Tanks

On April 17, 1989, tens of thousands of university students gathered spontaneously in Tiananmen Square, Beijing, China, calling for Freedom of the Press and political reform in that authoritarian Communist State.

By April 27, an estimated one in ten Beijing residents joined in the protests. Fearing that the unrest might lead to revolution, the Chinese Communist Politburo approved martial law on May 18.

On May 20, Peoples Liberation Army troops attempted to enter Tiananmen Square and disband the protestors to no avail.

On May 24, the PLA withdrew. The protests continued, raising speculation as to whether a change in government leadership might be in the offing.

On June 2, party elders approved use of military force to end the protests.

On June 3, PLA soldiers accompanied by armored vehicles and tanks fired on civilians with AK-47 rifles.

On June 4, the soldiers occupied Tiananmen Square. Parents of student protestors attempted to reenter the square via Chang 'an Boulevard were repulsed with live ammunition. When rescue workers tried to aid the fallen they were shot.

Overall, some 2,600 people were killed in this historic demonstration of intolerance for political dissent.

On the morning of June 5, the PLA had regained control of Beijing and the hunt for protestors to incarcerate and execute continued in earnest.

As a tank column moved forward along Chang 'an Boulevard, a young man carrying shopping bags stood in from of the lead tank. At first, the tank maneuvered to pass the young man but each time he repositioned himself to stand in front of the tank.

Failing repeatedly to get around him, the tank stopped and the driver turned off the motor. Then the young man climbed atop the tank and tried to talk to the driver.

Several other people then rushed from the side of the road to remove the young man from the way.

No one knows for sure what became of the young man, but the image of him standing peacefully and defiantly in front of that tank became an international symbol of freedom in the face of tyranny.

Tens of thousands of protesters were arrested and many were imprisoned. An unknown number were executed.

The ugly verities of Communism proved themselves to the world all over again.

President Ronald Reagan at the Brandenbutg Gate beseeching Mikhail Gorbechev to "Tear down this wall."

On August 13, 1961, the East German communist government, endeavoring to stem the increasing flow of East Germans to West Berlin and freedom, erected the infamous 87 mile long Berlin Wall that became a symbol of enslavement.

The Soviet Union demanded that the wall be constructed to put an end to an extraordinary exodus from East Germany (3.5 million defected before the wall was constructed).

The wall had 116 watchtowers along it with mounted machine guns, manned by GDR troops carrying automatic weapons.

A Different Point Of View

Mesh and signal fencing, anti-vehicle trenches, barbed wire, beds of nails, and German Shepherd dogs reinforced the wall's defenses against those who would be free.

A wide trench, known as a "death strip," was constructed and filled with raked gravel to reveal footprints.

On the death strip, kept free of visual obstacles to ensure a clear line of fire for the watchtower guards, over one hundred souls perished, preferring to risk death than to remain enslaved.

Once shot on the death strip, people were left to bleed to death. The guards prevented all rescue attempts.

On June 12, 1897, as political unrest began to rise in the Communist countries of Eastern Europe and the Soviet Union appeared incapable of suppressing moves for independence, President Ronald Reagon, against the wishes of his State Department, stood at the Brandedburg Gate and beseeched Soviet General Secretary Mikhail Gorbachev with these words: *"Mr. Gorgachev, tear town this wall!"*

President Reagon's speech was translated into German and broadcast through loud speakers to the East German side of the gate.

In 1989, the Soviet empire began to collapse as the bankruptcy of communism proved itself.

In September of 1989, civil unrest broke out across East Germany, causing the communist government to announce that it would relax limits on visitations between East German citizens and West German citizens in Berlin.

Then on October 18, 1989, East German dictator Erich Honecker resigned.

On November 4, a half million protestors gathered at Alexander Plaza to demonstrate against the government.

On November 9, chaos ensued within the East German government as large numbers of people began massing at border crossing points. Guards frantically called superiors seeking orders to stop passage but no official would authorize the use of force to prevent the exodus. The guards then opened checkpoints and thousands began pouring out of the communist East into the free West.

As the East German government made repeated concessions to ever increasing public demands and began to lose government control, people seeking freedom refused to wait, crossing the border in even greater numbers, doing so without permission and without resistance from the guards.

Beginning on the evening of November 9, 1989, and continuing for weeks thereafter, tens of thousands of people attacked the wall with hammers, chisels, and sledgehammers, breaking this symbol of oppression apart.

Finally, even the Brandenburg Gate was opened on December 22, 1989, the triumphant response to President Reagan's bold and courageous demand.

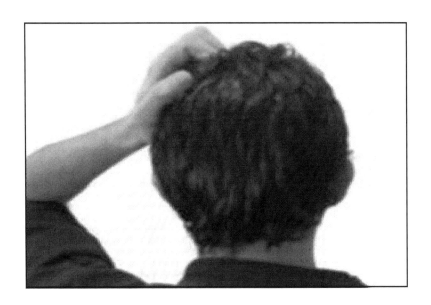

The New Distopia: 2011

The two greatest visions of a future dystopia were George Orwell's "1984" and Aldous Huxley's "Brave New World."

The debate, between those who watched our descent towards corporate totalitarianism, concerns who was right. Would we, as Orwell wrote, be dominated by a repressive surveillance and security state that used crude and violent forms of control? Or would we, as Huxley envisioned, be entranced by entertainment and spectacle, captivated by technology and seduced by profligate consumption to embrace our own oppression?

It turns out Orwell and Huxley were **both** right. Huxley saw the first stage of our enslavement; Orwell saw the second.

We have been gradually disempowered by a corporate state that has, as Huxley foresaw, seduced and manipulated us through sensual gratification, cheap mass-produced goods, boundless credit, political theater and amusement.

While we were being entertained, the regulations that once kept predatory corporate power in check were dismantled, the laws that once protected us have been rewritten and we are being impoverished. Now that credit is drying up, good jobs for the working class are gone forever, and mass-produced goods are becoming unaffordable, we find ourselves transported from "Brave New World" to "1984."

The state, crippled by massive deficits, endless war, and corporate malfeasance, is falling toward bankruptcy.

It is time for Big Brother to take over from Huxley's "feelies," the "orgy-porgy" and centrifugal "bumble-puppy." We are moving from a society where we are being skillfully manipulated by illusions and lies to one where we will be overtly controlled.

Orwell warned of a world where books were banned. **Huxley** warned of a world where no one **wanted** to read books.

Orwell warned of a state of permanent fear and war. **Huxley** warned of a culture diverted by mindless pleasure.

Orwell warned of a state where every conversation and thought was monitored and where dissent was brutally punished. **Huxley** warned of a state where a population, preoccupied by trivia and gossip, no longer cared about information or truth.

Orwell saw us *frightened* into submission. **Huxley** saw us *seduced* into submission.

Huxley, we are discovering, was but the prelude to Orwell.

Huxley understood the **process** by which we would be **complicit** in our own enslavement. **Orwell** understood the enslavement.

Now that the corporate coup is over, we stand defenseless and naked. We are beginning to **understand**, as Karl

Marx **knew**, that unfettered and unregulated capitalism is a brutal and revolutionary force that exploits human beings and the natural world, until exhaustion or collapse.

"The Party seeks power entirely for its own sake," Orwell wrote in "1984." "We are not interested in the good of others; we are interested solely in power. Not wealth or luxury or long life or happiness: only power; pure power. What pure power means you will understand presently. We are different from all the oligarchies of the past, in that we know what we are doing. All the others, even those who resembled ourselves, were cowards and hypocrites. The German Nazis and the Russian Communists came very close to us in their methods, but they never had the courage to recognize their own motives. They pretended, perhaps they even believed, that they had seized power unwillingly and for a limited time, and that just round the corner there lay a paradise where human beings would be equal and free. We are not like that. We know that no one ever seizes power with the intention of relinquishing it. **Power is not a means; it is an end.** One does not establish a dictatorship in order to safeguard a revolution; one makes the revolution in order to establish the dictatorship. The object of persecution is persecution. The object of torture is torture. The object of power is power."

The political philosopher Sheldon Wolin uses the term **"inverted totalitarianism"** in his book *Democracy Incorporated* to describe our political system. It is a term that would make sense to Huxley. In "inverted totalitarianism", the sophisticated technologies of corporate control, intimidation and mass manipulation, which far surpass those employed by previous totalitarian states, are effectively masked by the glitter, noise and abundance of a consumer society.

Political participation and civil liberties are gradually surrendered. The corporation state, hiding behind the smokescreen of the public relations industry, the entertainment industry, and the tawdry materialism of a consumer society, devours us from the inside out. It owes no allegiance to us or to the nation. It feasts upon our carcass.

The corporate state does not find its expression in a demagogue or charismatic leader. It is defined by the anonymity and facelessness of **"The Corporation"**.

The result is a one sided system of information. Celebrated courtiers, masquerading as journalists, experts and specialists, identify our problems and patiently explain imposed parameters. All those who argue outside the imposed parameters are dismissed as irrelevant cranks, extremists or members of a radical left. Prescient social critics are banished. Acceptable opinions have a range of only A to B. The culture, under the tutelage of these corporate courtiers, becomes, as Huxley noted, a world of cheerful conformity, as well as an endless and finally fatal optimism.

We busy ourselves buying products that promise to change our lives, make us more beautiful, confident or successful, as we are steadily stripped of rights, influence, and money. All the messages we receive through these systems of communication, promise a brighter, happier tomorrow. And this, as Wolin points out, is "the same ideology that invites corporate executives to exaggerate profits and conceal losses, but always with a sunny face." We have been entranced, as Wolin writes, by "continuous technological advances" that "encourage elaborate fantasies of individual prowess, eternal youthfulness, beauty through surgery, actions measured in nanoseconds: **a dream-laden culture of ever-expanding possibility and control,** whose denizens are prone to fantasies because the vast majority have imagination but little scientific knowledge."

Our manufacturing base has been dismantled. Speculators and swindlers have looted the U.S. Treasury and stolen billions from small shareholders who had set aside money for retirement or college. Civil liberties, including habeas corpus and protection from warrantless wiretapping, have been taken away. Basic services, including public education and health care, have been handed over to the corporations to exploit for profit. The few who raise voices of dissent, who refuse to engage in the **corporate happy talk**, are derided by the corporate establishment as freaks.

Attitudes and temperament have been cleverly engineered by the corporate state.

The façade is crumbling. And as more and more people realize that they have been used and robbed, we will move swiftly from Huxley's "Brave New World", to Orwell's "1984." The public, at some point, will have to face some very unpleasant truths. The good-paying jobs are not coming back. The largest deficits in human history mean that we are trapped in a **debt peonage system** that will be used by the corporate state to eradicate the last vestiges of social protection for citizens, including Social Security. The state has devolved from a capitalist democracy to neo-feudalism. And when these truths become apparent, anger will replace the corporate-imposed cheerful conformity. The bleakness of our post-industrial pockets, where some 40 million Americans live in a state of poverty and tens of millions in a category called "near poverty" — coupled with the lack of credit to save families from foreclosures, bank repossessions, and bankruptcy from medical bills — means that **"inverted totalitarianism"** will no longer work.

All excesses are justified in the titanic fight against evil personified.

The noose is tightening. The era of amusement is being replaced by the era of repression. Tens of millions of citizens have had their e-mails and phone records turned over to the government. We are the most monitored and spied-on citizenry in human history. Many of us have our daily routine caught on dozens of security cameras. Our proclivities and habits are recorded on the Internet. Our profiles are electronically generated. Our bodies are patted down at airports and filmed by scanners. And public service announcements, car inspection stickers, and public transportation posters constantly urge us to report suspicious activity to the State. The enemy is everywhere.

Those who do not comply with the dictates of the war on terror, a war which, as Orwell noted, is endless, are brutally silenced.

The FBI's targeting of antiwar and Palestinian activists, which in late September saw agents raid homes in Minneapolis and Chicago, is a harbinger of what is to come for all who dare defy the state's official **"Newspeak"**. The agents — our Thought Police — seized phones, computers, documents and other personal belongings. Subpoenas to appear before a grand jury have since been served on 26 people. The subpoenas cite federal law prohibiting "providing material support or resources to designated foreign terrorist organizations."

Terror, even for those who have nothing to do with terror, becomes the blunt instrument used by Big Brother to protect us from ourselves.

"Do you begin to see, then, what kind of world we are creating?" Orwell wrote. "It is the exact opposite of the stupid hedonistic Utopias that the old reformers imagined. A world of fear and treachery and torment, a world of trampling and being trampled upon, a world which will grow not less but more merciless as it refines itself."

Closing Statement

Why is there so little understanding of the distress of the nation today?

"For if after they have escaped the pollutions of the world through the knowledge of the Lord and Savior Jesus Christ, they are again entangled therein, and overcome, the latter end is worse that the beginning. For it had been better for them not to have known the way of righteousness, than, after they have known it, to turn from the holy commandment delivered unto them." — 2 Peter 2:20-21.

Is not this what has happened to America?
As far back as 1916, President Woodrow Wilson said:

"A great industrial nation is controlled by its system of credit. Our system of credit is concentrated. The growth of the nation, therefore, and all our activities are in the hands of a few men... We have come to be one of the worst ruled, one of the most completely controlled and dominated Governments in the civilized world — no longer a government of conviction and the vote of the majority, but a Government by the opinion and duress of small groups of dominant men."

Wilson must have been thinking of the Bankers of the non-federal Federal Reserve Bank.

Thomas Jefferson said:

"I believe that banking institutions are more dangerous to our liberties than standing armies. Already they have raised up a money aristocracy that has set the government at defiance. The issuing power [of money] should be taken from the banks and restored to the people to whom it properly belongs."

Abraham Lincoln declared:

"We have been the recipients of the choicest bounties of heaven. We have been preserved, these many years, in peace and prosperity. We have grown in numbers, wealth and power as no other nation has ever grown. But we have forgotten God. We have forgotten the gracious hand which preserved us in peace, and multiplied and enriched and strengthened us; and we have vainly imagined, in the deceitfulness of our hearts, that all these blessings were produced by some superior wisdom and virtue of our own. Intoxicated with unbroken success, we have become too self-sufficient to feel the necessity of redeeming and preserving grace too proud to pray to the God that made us! It behooves us, then, to humble ourselves before the offended Power, to confess our national sins, and to pray for clemency and forgiveness." — Lincoln's Proclamation for a National Day of Fasting, Humiliation and Prayer, April 30, 1893.

We are now living in the very end of **"the times of the end"** when Divine intervention will soon be manifest in the affairs of the nations of the world.

Epilogue

We are each born with a yearning to be free.

When government presumes to direct our lives, take our property, and rob us of the fruits of our labor, we are no better off than slaves.

From each of the foregoing examples, we learn precious lessons about freedom from those who have been deprived of it.

We now face in our own country a federal government that presumes to direct an ever greater amount of our daily lives, that is taking control over ever greater amounts of our property, and that is denying us an ever increasing quantity of the fruits of our labor.

Freedom is hunted down by government as an enemy of the centralized power of the State.

We must defend our freedom against this assault.

We should heed the words of President Ronald Reagan who warned us that:

"Freedom is never more that one generation away from extinction. We didn't pass it to our children in the bloodstream. It must be fought for, protected, and handed on for them to do the same."

Food For Thought

End Of Liberty
http://tinyurl.com/2axmemv

Police State 4

http://tinyurl.com/28l2kus

EndGame

http://tinyurl.com/yk4futp

Fall of the Republic
http://tinyurl.com/yho94je

The following documentary, *The Ring Of Power,* is in my opinion the best to watch on the Internet if you want a crash course on the power structure of the international banking elite. The power structure didn't happen overnight. It was created over a period of nearly 3,000 years; to the present past.

At least 95 percent of the info presented here is the truth. There is no doubt that we are living under the rule of the Empire of three City States: the Vatican City in Rome Italy; the City of London in London England; and the District of Columbia in the United States.

Ring Of Power

"On May 4th, 1970, America got a wake-up call. Six peaceful anti-war student demonstrators from Kent State in Jackson State University were shot dead by United States armed guards while dozens of others were wounded — the power of the United States military could turn its weapons on its own citizens."

Ring Of Power

"Only one nation in the world has been insane enough to drop atomic weapons of mass destruction on the innocent population of two large Japanese cities; chemical weapons of mass destruction on innocent civilians in Vietnam; and depleted radio-active uranium weapons of mass destruction on the people of Iraq."

Ring Of Power

"President Taft's 17th Amendment to the United States Constitution guaranteed the right of big money insiders to hand pick Senators and buy control of the United States Senate."

Ring Of Power

1. Present Past
http://tinyurl.com/2u2wt9d
2. Only the Start
http://tinyurl.com/2uajly2
3. Profiting from 911
http://tinyurl.com/345b68g
4. Hidden Empire
http://tinyurl.com/39yyg9e
5. Vatican Hoarding
http://tinyurl.com/3xhe2b6
6. Amen Pharaohs
http://tinyurl.com/3afruwx
7. Forbidden Link
http://tinyurl.com/39fbqto
8. Oceans of Blood
http://tinyurl.com/33bkksw
9. The Queen
http://tinyurl.com/37emjos
10. King of Kings
http://tinyurl.com/36htloh
11. The Empire
http://tinyurl.com/32m8ywh
12. The Cult of Amen
http://tinyurl.com/2vjmymk
13. Committee of 300
http://tinyurl.com/34qfenx
14. Godfathers
http://tinyurl.com/34aav4n

15. New World Order
http://tinyurl.com/34cyfnr
16. Freemason Mafia
http://tinyurl.com/3yszn39
17. Control All Money
http://tinyurl.com/358hcog
18. Credit Monopoly
http://tinyurl.com/328eky5
19. Blank Title
http://tinyurl.com/2uevdrw
20. Palestine Israel
http://tinyurl.com/37tevs5
21. The Butchers
http://tinyurl.com/39strh4
22. Asses of Evil
http://tinyurl.com/2u9eodp
23. Drug Running
http://tinyurl.com/34efg3u
24. War on Terror
http://tinyurl.com/352xt2c
25. Missing Episode
http://tinyurl.com/3yjkvgr
26. Antichrist
http://tinyurl.com/3x8gpq7
27. Credit Enslavement
http://tinyurl.com/362jodz
28. Tax Enslavement
http://tinyurl.com/32s5dp9
29. The Power
http://tinyurl.com/37qtsyn

Note the following closing words in:
From Debt To Prosperity
http://tinyurl.com/2vjgqay

The point to remember is this: The present financial system which creates money as debt, is the Financiers main means of establishing a one-world government. Debt Finance is the bridge that leads us from a free society to a dictatorship.

The only thing the Financiers fear, and the only thing that can stop them in their plan of world conquest, is the reform of the present financial system — the establishment of an honest ***debt-free-money System*** along the lines of the Social Credit Philosophy — when one realizes the importance of the Social Credit Solution and of spreading it and making it known.

This is why Soviet Foreign Minister Molotov said to Dr. Hewlett Johnson, Archbishop of Canterbury — in the 30's:

"We know all about Social Credit. It is the one theory in the world that we fear."

Social Credit Counterfeited

The redistribution of capital through bailouts on a global scale, i.e. with large corporations taking over the national capital of a country, has a purpose. To liquidate all national sovereignty with the clear intent to enslave every nation to the international Financiers who are attempting to control the whole world.

The main elements of their attempt seems, at first glance, to be very similar to the Social Credit proposals defined in *From Debt To Prosperity: 'Social Credit' Defined*. However, a system where each person is a slave to a world government is a far cry from what the philosophy of Social Credit in the book advocates.

One of the 18 Powers that "we the people" gave to Congress under the Constitution for the United States was the power "To borrow money on the credit of the United States." (Article 2, Section 8).

In other words, the power "To borrow money on the credit of [we the people of] the United States", — i.e. on the credit of the "citizens" of the United States.

In other words, on the Credit of the Society comprising the United States, — i.e. "Society's Credit."

Social Credit offers a unique way to finance the money system of the United States that would free society from purely financial problems and concerns.

Today, when there is no money, municipalities lay aside urgent works needed and requested by society, postponed or left undone, even though there is everything needed — workers and materials — to carry out these works.

Using Society's Credit would change all of this. It would make money a simple servant, a mere bookkeeping system — but a just one — in keeping with existing conditions.

Money would come into being as production is made, and money would disappear as production disappears.

Today, the production system does not distribute purchasing power directly to everyone. It distributes it only to those who are employed in production. And the more the production comes from the machine, the less it comes from human labor. Production even increases; whereas required employment decreases. So there is a conflict between progress and the system. Progress eliminates the need for human labor, while the system distributes purchasing power only to the employed, leaving the unemployed dependent on welfare to survive.

Our Declaration of Independence declares that "all Men are endowed by their Creator with certain unalienable rights, that among these are Life, Liberty, and the Pursuit of Happiness. That to secure these rights, Governments are instituted among Men, deriving their just Powers from the Consent of the Governed."

Everyone has the God given right to live, even those who are not employed. This is why, without in any way disturbing the system of reward for work, the use of Society's Credit (often defined as Social Credit) would distribute to every individual a periodical income, called a "social dividend."

This "dividend" would allow everyone to enjoy the fruits of progress without shame.

A Counterfeit is proposed:

The United States convened in a special global summit in September of 2000, establishing a new Charter for what they called "Global Democracy". It was signed by leaders from 56 nations as well as many private Non-Government Organizations (NGOs).

Economist John Kenneth Galbraith analyzed this Charter and said that it will implement laws in which each UN member "must surrender their sovereignty to the world body."

The charter calls for the integration of all corporations and financial institutions and the elimination of private corporate rights.

The laws make sure that every country will lose its sovereignty and national government.

The charter calls for the cancellation of all debt owned by the poorest nations, global poverty reductions, and the "equitable sharing of all global resources." Here they *too* speak about a national dividend to each citizen.

However, according to the G7 meeting in 1995 which introduced a Charter entitled *"People of the World,"* the proposition of a national dividend would fall under the dictatorship of a *Global Resource Bank* manned by the IMF and the World Bank, — instead of an American *Federal Credit Commission* and *National Credit Account* proposed by the Social Credit plan.

Article 2 of the United Nations Charter states, "Free access to the World Bank is by telecommunication." This means that all transactions would be made electronically; with the result of total control of all financial transactions by the IMF and the World Bank.

The unamerican "dividend" itself would be in the form of electronic money, with a microchip (or bio-sensor) implanted under the skin of each individual. Every form of production would be taken over by the New World Government and each citizen would be forced to turn to these "rulers of the world" in a cashless society for sustenance and support.

Contrariwise: The Social Doctrine of the Christian Church (which is Social Credit applied) gives us principles of justice that allows every man, woman and child the right to live, to have a part of all the natural resources and fruits of our modern technology, handed down from past generations, and the true freedom that those resources entail.

We must inform the people that they have been lied to by the very people that they have trusted to run their countries: the governments who have sold their citizens and nations to the financial moguls of today.

"...in the latter times some shall <u>depart from the faith</u>, giving heed to seducing spirits, and doctrines of devils; speaking lies in hypocricy; having their conscience seared with a hot iron." — I timothy 4:1,2.

*"On Christ, on solid ground I stand;
All other ground is sinking sand."*

*God's supply is greater than your demand;
security rests upon our good God's Grace.*

*We're being borne on eagles' wings;
God rewards you for trusting in his Care.*

Other Publications

NESARA: National *Economic Security and Reformation Act*
http://tinyurl.com/c8u42q6

History of Banking: *An Asian Perspective*
http://tinyurl.com/boeehjl

The People's Voice: *Former Arizona Sheriff Richard Mack*
http://tinyurl.com/d62fyg3

Asset Protection: *Pure Trust Organizations*
http://tinyurl.com/btrjfqp

The Matrix As It Is: *A Different Point Of View*
http://tinyurl.com/ckrbkge

From Debt To Prosperity: *'Social Credit' Defined*
http://tinyurl.com/d2tjmw3

Give Yourself Credit: *Money Doesn't Grow On Trees*
http://tinyurl.com/d7tphuv

My Home Is My Castle: *Beware Of The Dog*
http://tinyurl.com/bmzxc2n

Commercial Redemption: *The Hidden Truth*
http://tinyurl.com/d9etg7w

Hardcore Redemption-In-Law: *Commercial Freedom And Release*
http://tinyurl.com/cl65vrz

Oil Beneath Our Feet: *America's Energy Non-Crisis*
http://tinyurl.com/btlzqxf

Untold History Of America: *Let The Truth Be Told*
http://tinyurl.com/bu9kjjc

Debtocracy: *& Odious Debt Explained*
http://tinyurl.com/cooqzuz

New Beginning Study Course: *Connect The Dots And See*
http://tinyurl.com/cxpk42p

Monitions of a Mountain Man: *Manna, Money, & Me*
http://tinyurl.com/cusgcqs

Maine Street Miracle: *Saving Yourself And America*
http://tinyurl.com/d4yktlw

Reclaim Your Sovereignty: *Take Back Your Christian Name*
http://tinyurl.com/cf5taxh

Gun Carry In The USA: Your Right To Self-defence
http://tinyurl.com/cdn3y3y

Climategate Debunked: *Big Brother, Main Stream Media*
http://tinyurl.com/d6gy2xz

Epistle to the Americans I: *What you don't know about The Income Tax*
http://tinyurl.com/d99ujzm

Epistle to the Americans II: *What you don't know about American History*
http://tinyurl.com/cnyghyz

Epistle to the Americans III: *What you don't know about Money*
http://tinyurl.com/cp8nrh8

Made in the USA
Columbia, SC
05 November 2023